Rhythm

This book analyses the conceptual and concrete relationships between rhythm and law.

Rhythm is the unfolding of ordered and regulated movement. Law operates through the ordering and regulation of movement. Adopting a *rhythmanalytical* perspective – which treats natural and social phenomena in terms of their rhythms, repetitions, motions, and movements – this book offers an account of how legal institutions and practices can be theorised and explained in terms of rhythm. It demonstrates how the category of rhythm has jurisprudential significance – from the way Plato envisaged the functioning of the city-state, to the operation of the common law, as well as in our relationship to contemporary digital technology. In music, rhythm "orders" the movement of sound, binding together the motions and vibrations of sound in a way that is neither pure noise nor pure mechanics. In this way, rhythm can be deployed as a concept in the analysis of one of the central purposes of legal institutions and practices: to order the movements of bodies, whether the bodies of citizens in everyday life or of prisoners in rituals of punishment. This book engages with the mutual intersections and points of illumination between rhythm and law, such as ritual, measure, order, and change.

This book is an experimental *rhythmanalysis* of law, offering conceptual and methodological starting points, as well as proposing directions that could be deployed in future research. It is aimed primarily at legal scholars intrigued by rhythmanalysis and rhythmanalysts more generally. This book will also be of interest to those in the fields of philosophy, political and legal theory, sociology, and other social sciences.

Conor Heaney is Lecturer in Legal Theory/Law & Society in the Law School, University of Strathclyde, Glasgow, UK.

Part of the NEW TRAJECTORIES IN LAW
series editors
Adam Gearey, Birkbeck College, University of London
Prabha Kotiswaran, Kings College London
Colin Perrin, Commissioning Editor, Routledge
Mariana Valverde, University of Toronto

For information about the series and details of previous and forthcoming titles, see www.routledge.com/New-Trajectories-in-Law/book-series/NTL

A GlassHouse Book

Rhythm

New Trajectories in Law

Conor Heaney

Routledge
Taylor & Francis Group
a GlassHouse Book

First published 2023
by Routledge
4 Park Square, Milton Park, Abingdon, Oxon OX14 4RN

and by Routledge
605 Third Avenue, New York, NY 10158

Routledge is an imprint of the Taylor & Francis Group, an informa business

A GlassHouse book

British Library Cataloguing-in-Publication Data
A catalogue record for this book is available from the British Library

ISBN: 978-1-032-01658-0 (hbk)
ISBN: 978-1-032-39547-0 (pbk)
ISBN: 978-1-003-35023-1 (ebk)

DOI: 10.4324/9781003350231

Typeset in Bembo
by Apex CoVantage, LLC

Contents

Acknowledgements

Whenever one begins to think about writing acknowledgements, it becomes increasingly apparent that no projects take place in isolation and that the successful completion of any such work is possible only in the context of deep networks of support keeping everyday life afloat. The work for this book began in earnest around February 2020, and so this research unintentionally become a key distraction and obligation over the course of successive lockdowns. During this intense period, no stability or progress would have been possible without the daily love and support of my partner, Kamila, or without that of my parents, to whom my incalculable debts only grow exponentially. Special mentions must, of course, go to Nicola, Alfie, Lily-Rose, and (last, but not least) Czarnuszka.

Beyond this, I simply cannot omit expressing my deep gratitude to Connal Parsley, who provided not only the impetus and initial conversation that convinced me to write this book in the first place via a chance encounter on a train from St Pancras to Kent in February 2020, but also supportive conversation and endless advice over the ensuing years. Colin Perrin was also a supportive and open editor who was hugely encouraging in this process. Conor Crummey also offered, on more than one occasion, constructive listening to some of my more incoherent ramblings on this project. Finally, I would like to thank Jonjo Brady, Robert Porter, and all the attendees of *The Art of Everyday Life* seminar series who were generous enough to listen to me exploring some of these ideas in process.

Abbreviations

Laws.   Plato. 2016. *The Laws.* Ed. M. Schofield. Trans. T. Griffith. Cambridge: Cambridge University Press.

Tim.   Cornford. F. 1997. *Plato's Cosmology: The* Timaeus *of Plato.* Indianapolis/Cambridge: Hackett Publishing Company.

Introduction

The Clock, the Monastery, and the Prison Timetable

§1 Repeating

This is a book about approaching the nature of legal institutions, practices, and processes through the concept of rhythm. This *rhythmanalytical* approach to law has explanatory and epistemological purchase, and it is critically and politically significant. For introductory purposes, we can approach rhythm through thinking about how we experience and identify patterns in temporal processes. When listening to a song, we (sonically, vibrationally) experience the repetition of elements in the context of flux and flow such that these experiences are given a temporal "shape". The shape of vibrations in time is the rhythm. Rhythm is temporal and aesthetic (related to experience and affect), and it is also subject to formal study and abstraction: rhythm moves between the most abstract and intellectualised and the most embodied, emotional, and unconscious. Think about the Benedictine monks that Lewis Mumford (2010: 13) gestures towards in the following quote, whose devotional practices were repeated in a daily cycle:

> Opposed to the erratic fluctuations and pulsations of the worldly life was the iron discipline of the rule. Benedict added a seventh period to the devotions of the day, and in the seventh century, by a bull of Pope Sabinianus, it was decreed that the bells of the monastery be rung seven times in the twenty-four hours. These punctuation marks in the day were known as the canonical hours, and some means of keeping count of them and ensuring their regular repetition became necessary.

The bells of the monastery would ring, functioning as signal of devotional duty for monks to repeat the religio-aesthetic practice of prayer.

DOI: 10.4324/9781003350231-1

This sonic and temporal signal gave form and rhythm to everyday life in the monastery. At the abstract level, our technical capabilities have become increasingly devoted to developing technologies for measuring time (from the sundial, to the mechanical clock, to the contemporary atomic clock) through which our institutions regulate and produce social time. Our bodies are tuned by circadian rhythms themselves co-evolved with the daily rhythmic cycles of the Earth with the Sun. Rhythm thereby places us in the contexts of cosmology, ecology, biology, and theology, and sometimes all at once, given the Sun's historical religious significance in the regulation of daily, seasonal, and annual cycles.

How, then, do we get from rhythm to law? By approaching law *through* rhythm and thereby conceptualising law rhythmically, we do not treat law as a discrete social zone which can be isolated from the broader context a consideration of rhythm puts us in (e.g. cosmology, ecology, biology, etc.). Law is in operation when there is the attempted synchronisation and harmonisation of social flows, consolidating those social habits (e.g., custom) which order expectation frameworks in everyday life, as well as providing expectation frameworks for when those social habits are themselves frustrated (e.g., rituals of dispute resolution). Our rhythmanalysis of law centralises those previously mentioned *temporal* and *aesthetic* components at the forefront. For introductory purposes, we will say a little on what we point towards when using each of these terms.

On the *temporal* dimension, the law is full of temporal ideas, concepts, and practices, including the following examples. *Due process* names a particular temporal sequence or steps which liberal institutions designate as necessary for the operation of the *rule of law*, the proper *separation of powers*, and so forth. We can assess the extent to which legal processes are just or not through how they regulate and govern our movements in time, as with *fair trial rights* or *fair procedures*, which Conor Crummey (2020) has argued can function as an important aspect of participatory democratic citizenship. The temporality of procedure in lawmaking is suggested by some to constitute a criterion of legal validity and legitimacy (Manderson, 2000: 74; Raz, 1979). In common law systems, the adjudicative principle of *precedent* binds together past, present, and future, establishing the temporal continuum of the legal system; the common law 'synthesizes past, present, and future; its temporal movements forge the basis of its authority' (Mawani, 2015: 256). In Michel Foucault's famous opening passage of *Discipline and Punish* (1991: 3–7), a contrast is drawn between the methodical public torture (and burning) of Damiens in late 18th century Paris and the prison timetable schedule for prisoners as drawn up and imagined by Léon Faucher's (1838: 274–282) text on prison reform. While the former is a spectacular and violent public spectacle of punishment, the latter describes a vision of punishment defined by strict regularity and repetition, a cycle of daily activities (including prayer, work, and schooling) detailing prescribed quotidian rhythms for prison life. Key components of this contrast are the vastly distinct ways in which these different forms of punishment organise and order the movements and experiences of the judged through time. Following his attempted regicide, Damiens's torture and execution were temporally concentrated in an intense and excruciating day (28 March 1757), while the prison timetable is a temporally stretched cycle to be repeated for as long as is demanded by the judicial system. The prison sentence is a quantitative marker for the duration of liberty-deprivation, but the subjective experience of long-term prison sentences can transform and warp the sense of time. As Alyson Brown (1998: 97–98) notes, the everyday cycle of activities of continuous and ceaseless repetition can deprive 'prison time of meaning', merging 'all the days into an extended present'. This extension of the present is coupled with a change in how the past is remembered (as ever more remote) as well as how the future is imagined (as a fantasy of escape, or as something to repress). Regarding Foucault's contrast, these are principally different modalities of social repetition, two temporal rituals of punishment. These distinct penal styles are distinct rhythms of punishment, different methods of juridico-motional regulation from distinct milieus: they seek to institute *order* in their different ways. Whether it is the rituals of legal process, the performances of the trial, or the timetables of punishment, law temporally orders the movements of bodies and institutes social habits, adjudicating upon transgressions.

The second dimension of law opened through its rhythmic conceptualisation is its *aesthetic* one. In some legal theory, this aesthetic dimension is often given its sense through using the realm of art and literature as providing analytically useful comparisons (as simile or metaphor). Most famously, Ronald Dworkin's *legal interpretivism* founds itself on such comparisons. Conceiving of the law as a chain novel, each judge is imagined 'like a novelist in the chain' whose contributions to the law are ones that must *fit* with the legal genre and must also interpret and contribute to it in the 'best possible way'

(Dworkin, 1982: 193; 184; Kingwell, 1994). As Dworkin emphasises, this entrance of aesthetics into law is not meant in any way to
entangle the domains of law and aesthetics too deeply: 'law, unlike
literature, is not an artistic enterprise. Law is a political enterprise'
(Dworkin, 1982: 194). We agree with Desmond Manderson that
Dworkin does not appear to take the aesthetic comparison all too
seriously, remaining as it does at the level of *comparison* (implying a
relatively strict separation between law and aesthetics); instead, our
approach entangles the legal and the aesthetic: 'aesthetics is already
in the law' (Manderson, 2000: 31). This is not, as it may sound to
some, a demotion of law to "mere" aesthetics. As we have already
hinted, aesthetics (as from its Ancient Greek root αἴσθησῐς [aísthēsis],
meaning *perception* or *sensation*) in fact pertains to the entire domain
of what is sensed and felt, limited not just to language but to myriad
forms of communication (such as linguistic and symbolic), engaging our affective, emotional, and unconscious capacities, as well as
our rational, sense-making ones. Law is communicated not simply
through language (written or spoken) but through gesture and the
movement of bodies, through non-linguistic sounds and participation in ceremony and ritual, and in the ways objects are spatially
arranged and navigated in time (such as the layout of the courtroom
and the architecture of the prison). As Norman W. Spaulding argues
(2013: 315, quoted in Parsley, 2021: 441), the American approach to
the notion of due process is one that is 'intimately bound up with the
location, design, and use of law's administrative space'. Legal institutions distribute social order via spatial quantities as well as kinetic
and temporal flows, forming how legal institutions are perceived
and experienced. While realms of art are *particular* realms of aesthetic
experimentation with these quantities and flows, our milieus are
entirely aesthetic vibrational continuums.

Two clarificatory examples of the aesthetics of both punishment
and judgment follow. The torture of Damiens, as depicted by Foucault, was a public spectacle (public spectatorship being a crucial factor), and punishment often included various symbolisms. (Foucault
mentions the piercing of the tongue of blasphemers, as well as Damiens holding in his 'guilty right hand the famous dagger with which
he had committed the crime' [1991: 45].) Such symbolisms perform
political functions, where an injury to the sovereign (the crime) is
reciprocated back onto the body of the subject who violated the law
in ways that are often *imitations* of the original crime: the punishment
is both temporally concentrated (on a particular day) and spatially

concentrated (in a particular place) for the purposes of restitution and the restoration of juridico-political power. Faucher's prison timetable just a few decades later evidences transformations in the imagined politics, aesthetics, and temporalities of punishment, with the publicity shifting *away from* the punishment and *towards* the trial (1991: 9), where the condemned are increasingly hidden from society in order to be "corrected" via, amongst other things, the timetable. The rhythmic cycle of the timetable is constituted at the intersections of temporality and aesthetics: activities are organised and separated by drum rolls (an aesthetic signal) at specific intervals in which tasks are to be completed, with order and silence among prisoners being maintained. The soundscape of the courtroom is also of note here, as well as the ritualistic links between sounds and movements therein: consider even the small example of the three raps on the bench which prefigure a verbal formulation to announce the entrance into the Court Number One at the Old Bailey by the judge (Grant, 2019). For our purposes, the important point to highlight is the manner in which legal practices are infused with aesthetic symbolisms, rituals, and various forms of choreography which order the movements of our bodies as well as distribute who should speak, when they should speak, what they should say, how they should be punished and for how long. We saw already how aesthetic criteria play a role in legal judgment in Dworkin's interpretivism, but it is not uncommon for legal judgment itself to be imagined like a musical note which ought to *fit* and thereby contribute to the *harmony* of the legal system. For example, in *Patel v Mirza*, Lord Toulson (at para. 99) famously noted that a central reason for the common law approach to the doctrine of illegality as a defence to a civil claim was that the law 'should be coherent and not self-defeating' so as not to allow 'inconsistency and disharmony in the law, and so cause damage to the integrity of the legal system' (para. 100). Therein, Lord Sumption also cited with approval McLachlin J's judgment for the Canadian Supreme Court in *Hall v Hebert*, noting (at para. 230) that the law's 'internal coherence requires that contract, tort and criminal law should be in harmony'. The legal process is a juridico-aesthetic social performance with such choreographies throughout, from arrest to judgment to punishment: the aesthetics of punishment and judgment are neither secondary nor subsequent.

We can speak in more general terms on the aesthetics and temporality of law in everyday life through the notion of *order*. In everyday life, the ordering of movements is learned and habituated to in relationship with various social institutions and life periods (such as childhood, work-life, and retirement). *Order* is socially distributed through time-management and time-discipline techniques via social institutions which, if consistently and generally adhered to, produce a certain mode of social stability glued by shared social practices. When we see the terms *law* and *order* conceptually coupled, it is precisely in the sense that law names those institutions indissociable from the attempt to distribute order upon the movements of its environment (or *milieu*) – the movements and flows of bodies and their voices, of goods, of capital, and so on. Law produces certain practices, expectations, and frameworks constitutive of the temporality of the milieu. Time is that through which law orders the movements of bodies, but this is not unique to law.

In the opening quote in this Introduction, from a famous section titled "The Monastery and the Clock" early in his 1934 text *Technics and Civilization*, Lewis Mumford highlights an innovation in time-measurement and time-management which served to synchronise the actions of Benedictine monks. The temporal regulation of devotional hours created a framework of practices and expectations about ordered conduct in the monastery for the purposes of proper comportment and, through this, a hoped-for aesthetic synchronisation with theological order (a hoped-for experience of the divine, or as close as is possible to it for salvation). E. P. Thompson's 1967 "Time, Work-Discipline, and Industrial Capitalism" describes the shifting labour rhythms marking the many transitions demanded by forces of industrial capitalism, highlighting what is an evolution of the technique deployed by the Benedictine monks. Taking the example of the *Law Book of the Crowley Iron Works*, which Thompson describes as an 'entire civil and penal code . . . to govern and regulate [Crowley's] refractory labour-force' (1967: 81) (Crowley ran large-scale ironworks), it therein describes the regulation of time-usage through monitoring and the attendant application of monetary deductions (primarily by the Monitor and Warden of the Mill). In addition, the *Law Book* mentions the Warden's responsibilities in a manner analogous to those who rang the bells of the monastery at canonical hours, or to the prison timetable's drum roll. Whereas the bells of the canonical hours were calls to synchronise with *theological order*, the drum rolls of the prison calls to *legal order*, the bells of the workplace functioned as calls to *industrial capitalist order.*

Every morning at 5 a clock the Warden is to ring the bell for beginning to work, at eight a clock for breakfast, for half an hour

after work again, at twelve a clock for dinner, at one to work and
at eight to work ring for leaving work and all to be lock'd up.

(Thompson, 1967: 82)

By 1700, these techniques of temporal regulation marked by industrial
capitalism were clearly emerging, which Mumford will trace back to
the monastery:

> If the mechanical clock did not appear until the cities of the thir-
> teenth century demanded an orderly routine, the habit of order
> itself and the earnest regulation of time-sequences had become
> almost second nature in the monastery. . . . So one is not straining
> the facts when one suggests that the monasteries – at one time
> there were 40,000 under the Benedictine rule – helped to give
> human enterprise the regular collective beat and rhythm of the
> machine; for the clock is not merely a means of keeping track of
> the hours, but of synchronizing the actions of men.

(2010: 13–14)

Given this, it is of course no surprise that, for example, within weeks
(or even days) after seizing control of the Cape of Good Hope in the
British colonial push to establish control of South Africa, a British time
signal was installed, and that each day at noon cannon fire functioned
as the call to *colonial order*. As well as highlighting this, David Rooney
provides the further example of the 'energetic program of clock tower
building' established by British colonisers in south-eastern Australia
from the 1820s onwards in the inculcation of 'Western ideas of discipline and order' (2021: 20). As is well known by those who govern,
time functions to regulate, synchronise, and measure human action
(or, better yet, in our own self-regulation and self-measurement). It
functions in the imposition, transmission, or distribution of an *ordered
sequence of movements:* rhythm. For Henri Lefebvre, political power is
totally entangled with such ordering:

> Political power knows how to use and manipulate time, dates,
> time-tables. It combines the unfurlings [*déploiements*] of those
> that it employs (individuals, groups, entire societies), and rhythms
> them. This is officially called mobilisation. The authorities have to
> know the polyrhythmia of the social body that they set in motion.

(Lefebvre, 2013: 78)

The rhythmisation of the movements of bodies, voices, and souls through law is our central theme, but in exploring this, we will come into contact with the ways in which images of order and rhythm in law so often themselves are thought to be important insofar as they *synchronise* with other social and natural rhythms. At this point, and bringing this introduction towards its conclusion, we will now make some more general methodological points about the analytical approach of this book, as well as its form, content, and purposes.

§2 Law and the Milieu (Methodological and Structural Notes)

This book is an experimental *rhythmanalysis* of law. Rhythmanalysis names a set of approaches or methods to the study of social, political, technological, and natural phenomena. While there is no one set or fixed way of doing rhythmanalysis, all rhythmanalyses – and this is our first methodological note – will pay particular attention to those *temporal* and *aesthetic* dimensions we have been highlighting.

Rhythmanalysis addresses the dynamic interactions between such phenomena with their broader context, a context we refer to with the term *milieu*. The *milieu* incorporates not just those factors concerning the physical environment, but the array of practices and institutions (including linguistic, economic, social, political, religious, medical, psychiatric, technological, and mediatic) which permeate, structure, and order everyday life. Legal institutions and practices emerge from their milieu, but this does not mean that the latter *determines* the former. Nor indeed the reverse: law does not *determine* the milieu. There are always dynamic interactions between them, strewn across the generations: law is here conceptualised as a *relatively* autonomous set of social practices of key significance in how this or that milieu carves the future. Through this dynamic between law and the milieu, law can work in the service of social reproduction as well as social transformation. This rhythmic interaction between law and the milieu we can call *recursive*. As Yi Chen notes, 'Recursive phenomena are at the heart of identifying rhythms' (2018: 4). Our second methodological note therefore states that legal institutions and practices are conditioned and produced by the milieu, and these institutions and practices in turn (recursively) condition and produce those milieus. Such recursive processes are never mere mechanical repetitions, as though law and the milieu were in a state of perpetual oscillating sameness (recursion cannot be grasped through the image of the *metronome*), but rather are in continuous processes of looping and change (Hui, 2019: 4). Recursions are less like metronomes or circles and more like spirals or folds. Change can, however, be subtle, and it can often be as much a methodological and conceptual risk to overstate the homogeneity of repetition as the heterogeneity of difference.

With these two brief methodological notes, we will now provide an indication of the structure of the text. This book has a continuous narrative and approach, but specific chapters are written to have a degree of independence which allows them to be approached separately and for different purposes. The reader is invited to navigate the text as they choose and for whatever might fit their purposes.

Chapter 1 will be focused primarily on introducing new readers to the literature surrounding the notion of rhythm more generally as well as the approach of rhythmanalysis more specifically. The discussion here will primarily be philosophical and methodological, grounding our approach to rhythmanalysis in the context of a more general understanding of the nature of social, political, technological, and natural phenomena, before offering some comments at the end of the chapter on a rhythmanalysis of *law*.

Chapter 2 will be a study on the intersections between rhythm and law in the late dialogues of Plato. Plato uses rhythm across numerous dialogues, by far the most in his *Laws*, and in many ways formed a new definition of the term that we still use. This chapter offers an account of the etymology of rhythm as well as a reading of Plato's analysis of the rhythm-law nexus, demonstrating the historical depth and scope of this book's investigation as well as seeking to contribute to the developing but still under-explored literature on the enduring richness of Plato's late dialogues for thinking about the intersections between cosmology, music, politics, and law.

Chapter 3 has two key aims, partly designed to address different potential readers of this book and address the "gaps" in the literature at the rhythm-law nexus. The first, to legal scholarship, seeks to offer an example of the potential purchase of rhythmanalysis to legal objects of analysis through a discussion of time-standardisation. The second, to rhythmanalysts, seeks to underline the significant import that analysis of legal institutions and practices has for enriching our thinking about rhythm and in the conceptualisation of everyday life. This will be attempted through elaborating the notion of *juridico-political continuity* via a discussion of both statute and common law.

This book thus seeks to underline the purchase of the *rhythmanalytical* approach as a mode of investigation and analysis into the understanding and transformation of everyday life, to help open up this approach to further transdisciplinary investigation and exchange, and to function as an invitation to the creation of new rhythmanalytical concepts and critiques.

References

Brown, A. 1998. 'Doing Time': The Extended Present of the Long-Term Prisoner. *Time & Society*, 7(1): 93–103.

Chen, Y. 2018. *Practising Rhythmanalysis: Theories and Methodologies*. London: Rowman & Littlefield.

Crummey, C. 2020. Why Fair Procedures Always Make a Difference. *Modern Law Review*, 83(6): 1221–1245.

Dworkin, R. 1982. Law as Interpretation. *Critical Inquiry*, 9(1): 179–200.

Faucher, L. 1838. *De la réforme des prisons*. Paris: Angé.

Foucault, M. 1991. *Discipline and Punish: The Birth of the Prison*. Trans. A. Sheridan. London: Penguin Books.

Grant, T. 2019. *Court Number One: The Old Bailey Trials that Defined Modern Britain*. London: John Murray.

Hall v Hebert [1993] 2 SCR 159.

Hui, Y. 2019. *Recursivity and Contingency*. London: Rowman & Littlefield International.

Kingwell, M. 1994. Let's Ask Again: Is Law Like Literature? *Yale Journal of Law & the Humanities*, 6(2): 317–352.

Lefebvre, H. 2013. *Rhythmanalysis: Space, Time and Everyday Life*. Trans. S. Elden and G. Moore. London: Bloomsbury Academic.

Manderson, D. 2000. *Songs without Music: Aesthetic Dimensions of Law and Justice*. Berkeley, CA: University of California Press.

Mawani, R. 2015. The Times of Law. *Law & Social Inquiry*, 40(1): 253–263.

Mumford, L. 2010. *Technics & Civilization*. Chicago, IL: The University of Chicago Press.

Parsley, C. 2021. Automating Authority: The Human and Automation in Legal Discourse on the Meaningful Human Control of Lethal Autonomous Weapons Systems. In *Routledge Handbook of International Law and the Humanities*. Eds. S. Chalmers and S. Pahuja. London: Routledge, pp. 432–445.

Patel v Mirza [2016] UKSC 42.

Raz, J. 1979. *The Authority of Law*. Oxford: Clarendon Press.

Rooney, D. 2021. *About Time: A History of Civilization in Twelve Clocks*. New York: W. W. Norton & Company.

Spaulding, N. W. 2013. The Enclosure of Justice: Courthouse Architecture, Due Process, and the Dead Metaphor of Trial. *Yale Journal of Law & the Humanities*, 24(1): 311–343.

Thompson, E. P. 1967. Time, Work-Discipline, and Industrial Capitalism. *Past & Present*, 38: 56–97.

1

Rhythm as Object and Principle

§3 Loop

Rhythm can be an elusive and enigmatic concept, but it is one with surprising richness, having an immediacy and concreteness bound up with
its relationship with the everyday. One's experience of everyday life is
indissociably rhythmic, involving as it does those activities we repeat,
repeat, and repeat, and through which we adapt and change according
to new circumstances which call for new habits and routines. Alfred
North Whitehead highlights how the notion of rhythm enables the
'conveyance of difference within a framework of repetition' (1967: 17),
but we could equally reverse the statement, and note that rhythm also
enables the conveyance of repetition within a framework of difference.

To take the example we opened with in the Introduction, through
the flux and flow of the living present when listening to musical
objects, we find that they are continuously self-differentiating, but
also continuously repeating through patterns, motifs, and loops. In
the musical object's temporal unfolding, it is as if the song is *sampling
itself*, looping in a decentred spiral whereby each repetition recon-
textualises what has passed and what is to come. Sampling is both a
technique of repetition and of creation. Paul D. Miller (aka DJ Spooky
that Subliminal Kid) evinces this when thinking of the creative elabo-
ration of ideas: 'Take the idea and fold it in on itself. Think of it as
laptop jazz, cybernetic jazz, nu-bop, ILLbient – a nameless, formless,
shapeless concept given structure by the rhythm' (2004: 25). This is
not limited to music: think of how *milieus* reproduce themselves (and
thereby transform) through the continual sampling of social practices.
The terms *tradition, custom,* and *ritual* denote social rhythms which, to
varying degrees, sample activities from the past in shaping the present
and future of that particular milieu. They denote practices through

DOI: 10.4324/9781003350231-2

which, to paraphrase Miller, a milieu takes an idea and/or practice, folds it in on itself, and gives (social) structure to the milieu through the rhythm this produces. Consider the traditions, customs, and rituals bound up with the ideas and practices of *democracy*; for example, periodic voting synchronised with electoral cycles. Elections are processes which reproduce the social structure and its institutions and can (however slightly) change the temporal direction that milieu takes. Democratic institutions *in practice* aid in the formation, reproduction, and transformation of social structures through their periodic rhythmisation of individuals towards the practice of voting, a procedure which functions as a ritual which cyclically (re-)establishes the legitimacy of the authority of those institutions, temporarily empowering some political actors while disempowering others. (We will go into more detail on this in §6.) We do *not* suggest rhythm is an aesthetic *metaphor* for the everyday, but rather underline how the everyday is itself aesthetic and rhythmic.

As we noted in §2, our focus here is to introduce readers to the variegated ways we can approach the concept of *rhythm* at a general level, as well as how these can be brought together through a *rhythmanalytical* methodology. In order to clarify the rhythmanalytical approach to law which will define the remaining chapters of this book, it is necessary for us first to highlight some angles through which we can go about approaching and doing rhythmanalysis. Readers of this chapter will thereby develop a sense of the transdisciplinary reach of rhythmanalysis, touching as it does on biology, cosmology, technology studies, history, sociology, politics, economics, and philosophy, and so forth. Discussion in §4 focuses on different "rhythm-objects" – that is, objects of analysis which can be approached rhythmically – in order to evidence this transdisciplinary reach. We are using the term "object" here for the purposes of consistency and clarity throughout the text, but it should be noted that rhythmanalysts have often been sceptical of characterising phenomena of study and analysis in terms of the rather static-sounding term *object*. Henri Lefebvre notes, 'The classic term in philosophy, "the object", is not appropriate to rhythm. "Objective"? Yes, but exceeding the narrow framework of objectivity, by bringing to it a multiplicity of (sensorial and significant) meanings' (2013: 41). We will not go into too much detail here. (More will be said in §5.1.) For our purposes, we will simply deploy the term "objects" for ease of use, but while highlighting that by framing these as *rhythm*-objects, we centralise the processual character of all phenomena of study.

After this, §5, using rhythm as a *principle* of analysis, will underline how rhythmanalysis is an approach which, instead of beginning with specific rhythm-objects, begins with concepts and categories capable of approaching these different rhythm-objects in a multilayered and multi-levelled approach. The contrast between §4 (rhythm as object) and §5 (rhythm as principle) is one which Lefebvre highlights (2013: 15) at the beginning of his late work titled *Rhythmanalysis: Space, Time and Everyday Life*, suggesting that we can study rhythm in two ways. First, we can use a "scientific" spirit by beginning with the concrete, comparing concrete cases (e.g., the rhythms of the human body), an approach which he associates closely with practice (e.g., the specialist practice of the doctor), and making generalisations thereon. This approach begins with rhythm-objects and develops practical principles from this study. The second way is through beginning with the abstract (concepts and categories of analysis and judgment) and engaging in some cautious speculation in relation to particular objects of reasoning. This approach therefore begins by developing principles of analysis *through which* to study the particular objects. For us, these two approaches are not mutually exclusive. Our approach will be characterised by continuous movement between the abstract (principles) and the concrete (objects).

In §6, we will discuss some practices, processes, and patterns in legal theory and practice amenable to rhythmanalysis or to analysis as rhythm-objects. As a shorthand, we will refer to these as *nomorhythmic objects* or *nomorhythms*, a term we develop through conjoining "rhythm" with *nomos*. *Nomos* (or *nomoi* in the plural) is broadly translated as "law" or "custom" (and Plato's *Laws*, which we discuss in the next chapter, is itself titled *Nómoi*). In discussions of Ancient Greek thought, it is common for *nomos* to be distinguished from *physis* (nature), and those in Ancient Greek thought who distinguished sharply between *nomos* and *physis* made a distinction comparable to the distinction between *nature* and *culture*. Of course, it is not quite so simple, but this will serve as a starting point. *Nomos* in the Ancient Greek (either νομός or νόμος depending on the sense and context) has a complex set of meanings, but for our purposes we can highlight three important senses (Liddell and Scott, 2017: 467). First, *nomos* pertains to the assigning, apportioning, or distribution (including in ritual forms) of *resources* and spatial portions, principally food and land. Call this the *distributive* dimension of nomos. Second, it pertains to the customs, conventions, or laws of a given territory, that is, all the *behaviours* and *practices* which can or ought to be performed by those within the sphere of the *nomos* or those which can be engaged in given existing legal forms. Legal institutions create conditions of action in a milieu, providing the background legal architecture that structures and orders social relations from, for example, the procedures for setting up a limited company to procedures of dispute resolution. Call this the *behavioural* and *regulatory* dimension of nomos. In this book, our focus will be on these two senses which we will at different points refer to as the distributive, behavioural, and regulatory dimensions of nomos. But it is important to highlight a third sense of the term. *Nomos* was also used in a musical sense, referring to a musical strain, song, or ode, referring to a "law" of music, such as a 'set of notes or intervals performed in certain sequences in a particular manner' (Fleming, 1977: 222–223) or perhaps linked with specific locations or festivals which constrained and regulated musico-poetic performance. This overlaps with behavioural and regulatory dimensions, but in a sense with a clearer relationship to musical aesthetics.

§4 Rhythm as Object

§4.1 Biorhythms

To call something a rhythm-object is to centre analytical attention on the ways in which that phenomena can be understood in terms of its temporal and aesthetic patterns. We are accustomed to thinking of artistic objects with and through rhythm, in music, poetry, and literature most particularly. However, our first class of rhythm-objects will be *biological*. We can call them *biorhythmic objects* and their patterns, *biorhythms*. The problems of time and rhythm are well-known in biology, not least in the study of evolution, but also in the field of chronobiology and through important research into biological rhythm. Indeed, Brian Goodwin (1996: 97) conceptualised organisms as 'essentially rhythmic systems accounting for the universality of biological clocks'.

In 1999, for example, one of the key papers in this field was published which evidenced that the human *circadian* rhythm – "circa" meaning *approximately*, "diem" meaning *day* – in terms of the sleep-wake cycle is closely synchronised to an Earth day, and that the human circadian pacemaker averages close to 24 hours in the absence of external cues. This research tested subjects in conditions where normal time cues are absent, namely, where there is highly controlled exposure to light and dark in what is called a *forced desynchrony protocol* (Czeisler et al., 1999;

also see Kelly et al., 1999; Siffre, 1975; Gentry et al., 2021). Circadian rhythms are ubiquitous on Earth: from bacteria, to algae, to slime mould, to plants, to animals. Given the evidence suggesting that this rhythm is able to persist (for at least some time) even when environmental factors are altered, there are grounds for suggesting that what chronobiologists call *endogenous pacemakers* exist in organisms. That is, that organisms have evolved – and successive generations inherit – relatively autonomous "body clocks" that can, to an extent, self-regulate. It is worth noting here that the 2017 Nobel Prize in Physiology or Medicine was awarded to Jeffrey C. Hall, Michael Rosbash, and Michael W. Young for their work on the *molecular* underpinnings of circadian rhythms through circadian oscillation in the fruit fly *Drosophila melanogaster*. Such work fortifies this view of the *endogeneity* of circadian rhythms.

By contrast, whenever behaviour relies upon or is explicitly synchronised with some external or environmental factor, these are called *exogenous zeitgebers*. *Zeitgeber* means time-giver or synchroniser. The circadian rhythms of everyday life of the organism are often regulated through the movement between endogenous pacemakers and exogenous zeitgebers. For example, with respect to the circadian rhythm of the sleep-wake cycle in humans, the central endogenous pacemaker is what is called the suprachiasmatic nucleus (SCN) (a group of neurons in the hypothalamus), and the most studied exogenous zeitgeber is light. Through the retinohypothalamic tract, SCN receives information on the exogenous zeitgeber of light, and this information will then in turn impact serotonin and melatonin levels via SCN's connection to the pineal gland. Less light will result in more melatonin secretion, aiding the organism's going to sleep. The input of light is often described as providing an exogenous "reset" to our internal body clocks, aiding in the regulation of daily sleep-wake cycle. Body temperature also follows a clear circadian rhythm (Refinetti and Menaker, 1992), and research has suggested that temperature's link to SCN is worthy of more study (Buhr et al., 2010).

In addition to the most well-known *circadian* rhythms (sleeping-waking, linked hormonal patterns, body temperature), two other biorhythms are worth mentioning. First, *infradian* rhythms have cycles longer than a day and include rhythms such as menstrual cycles or certain seasonal patterns in other animals (e.g., migration and hibernation). Second, *ultradian* rhythms have cycles shorter than a day, and the most common examples are the phases of the sleep cycle, blood circulation, or bowel activity. Our evolution has resulted in diurnal patterns (i.e., where activity tends to be during sunlight and rest at night), but evolution in other animals has resulted in nocturnal patterns. Our human cycles are indissociable from how we have historically related to the oscillation between the solar and the lunar: our biorhythms have historically evolved in relation to *cosmorhythms*, that is, cosmological rhythms. Some research has explored the potential plasticity of human circadian rhythms for the purpose of thinking about synchronising them with the Martian solar day-night and light-dark cycle for space exploration (Scheer et al., 2007). Such works are examples of approaching rhythm as an object of analysis, and using this to develop principles (e.g., medical or therapeutic) for practice. Other research in biological rhythm, for example, explores the ways in which night-shift work can lead to disruptions in the body's circadian rhythm, sleep deprivation, and reduced cognitive function. To give a final example in this domain, research has found correlations between altered circadian rhythms and depression, postulating the potential of forms of *chronotherapy* in response (Germain and Kupfer, 2008; Harvey, 2011; Baron and Reid, 2014).

§4.2 Cosmorhythms

Human biorhythms are entangled with cosmological rhythms or *cosmorhythms*. The most prominent being, of course, *solar rhythms*: our evolution is one in relative attunement to the particular timescapes produced through the Earth's position in the solar system and its production of the cycles of day-night, tides, seasons, and longer cycles (e.g., the approximately 11-year solar magnetic activity cycle, measured through the presence of sunspots). Lefebvre suggests that the origin of the notion of the cyclical is in fact these cosmic rhythms (2013: 18). The interplay between our endogenous pacemakers and exogenous zeitgebers is important to consider given that cosmorhythms are not perpetually the same and change our environmental conditions. The length of days on Earth changes throughout the solar year due to the tilt of the Earth's axis and its wobbly procession around the Sun. The different seasons this produces require different modes of activities for organisms to survive. Exogenous zeitgebers provide this crucial information for organisms to modify their behaviour in accord with what is required by environmental conditions. This is what is often termed a "phase shift" in circadian rhythm. The second most prominent conductors of Earth's biorhythms are *lunar rhythms*.

The tidal cycle, produced through the Moon's gravitational pull on Earth, lasts 24.8 hours. Due to geological factors (coastline shapes, land masses), tidal schedules can be highly irregular (Scofield, 2011: 117). Marine organisms in particular have absorbed and co-evolved with lunar rhythms, synchronising their feeding or reproductive cycles in relation to them (Scofield, 2011: 117–118).

§4.3 Technosocial Rhythms

Our rhythms of everyday life are by no means solely choreographed by the biorhythmic and the cosmorhythmic: sociotechnical processes are continuously changing and trying to put them in order. The example of contemporary shift-work mentioned previously makes sense only when situated in the history of industrial and post-industrial (24/7) capitalism and the ways it measures time and institutes social rhythms through techniques of measurement, governance, and punishment (whether economic or juridico-political). Technologies impact upon our everyday life through how they shift our habits, realigning how we distribute our attention, as well as the possibilities new technologies open up for the surveillance and control of such habits. Artificial light can, for example, function as an alternative *zeitgeber* in the sleep-wake cycle. Technology and its relation to the social context as such can also be discussed as another mode of rhythm-objects. Let us call these *technosocial rhythms*.

Bernard Stiegler uses the term *technical program* to describe the ways in which political and economic forces structure how technological developments are absorbed into the cycles of everyday life and through which our actions can be ordered, synchronised, and aligned: from technologies of transport, to time-measurement, to internet connectivity. To provide an example: if we take the previously mentioned transition from the sort of industrial capitalism discussed in the Introduction, we see how the technology of time-measurement allowed for synchronised action (whether in the monastery or in the workplace). The transition to digital capitalism is a technorhythmic transition: from analogue to digital technologies through emergence of *real time* (light speed) global communication, exchange, and networking (Stiegler, 2009: 89–94; 145; also see Lefebvre, 2013: 57). Everyday life could be said to move faster when digitalised, producing new technosocial rhythms (see Ikoniadou, 2012, 2014).

Technical programs, or technology and infrastructure more generally, are in the business of changing the environmental conditions of our everyday lives, 'shaping the preconditions under which we experience time's structure and its passage' (Edwards, 2003: 195). Mikko Jalas, Jenny Rinkinen, and Antti Silvast have, for example, researched Finnish infrastructures of electricity provision, focusing in particular on the contrast between electricity grid services and domestic wood-based heating systems. Well-functioning electricity infrastructure fades into the background of conscious awareness in everyday life, coming to the fore most particularly in the case of blackouts. As they put it, 'technological systems serve to isolate us from the cycles of nature' (Jalas et al., 2016: 18), and blackouts are cases where households become more exposed to these natural cycles. Conversely, whenever wood-based heating systems are in operation, this entails different patternings of social action, modes of planning, integrating infrastructure maintenance with one's other activities, and the management of 'two-year cycles of obtaining, drying and using firewood and the operation and maintenance of machinery therein' (Jalas et al., 2016: 19). In the context of electricity grid infrastructure, the regularity and relative stability of the service – and the organisation of which is subject to continuous legal regulation – provide a sense of sameness to everyday life, providing the space and time for households to choose these or those activities. In the context of wood-based heating systems, more continuous service and social labour is required for the maintenance of infrastructure, rhythmising the social body differently. This may mean less "free time", but it may also result in clearer structure and routine, the working together of households, and the potential strengthening of bonds of social solidarity whenever local communities engage in informal forms of mutual aid (Jalas et al., 2016: 20).

Our social evolution is tied to our relationship with technical objects as well as the social, legal, and political contexts which shape this relationship. If biological evolution incorporates processes of natural selection, then we can comparatively note that social and technical evolution incorporates processes of *artificial* selection. This is a term introduced by Stiegler indicating how our social and technical developments introduce new vectors into our evolutionary process and carve out a space through which we, at least partially, can influence our own futures (Moore, 2017: 193). This itself is a point Stiegler draws from André Leroi-Gourhan, who argued that technics marked a 'continuation of evolution by other means, with different techniques amounting to mutations external to the biological organism' (Moore, 2017: 197). The technical and social environment forms a field of *zeitgebers* in the rhythmising of our everyday lives.

Biorhythms, cosmorhythms, and *technosocial rhythms* each constitute distinct and complex sets of rhythm-objects, forming relatively independent fields of inquiry for different purposes and aims, from molecular biology, to anthropology, to science and technology studies, to political theory. No doubt, however, they all continually interact and are relevant in our own everyday lives, insofar as we have evolved and continually evolve with and as these biosocial, cosmosocial, and technosocial rhythms. It is this necessary polyrhythmic entangledness which motivates the rhythmanalytical approach, where rhythm becomes a principle of analysis that seeks to conceptualise the relations among them.

§5 Rhythm as Principle

§5.1 Three Common Threads in Rhythmanalysis

As Lefebvre notes (2013: 19), historically different thinkers have appeared tempted to make rhythm a principle of analysis, mentioning Friedrich Nietzsche (see Heaney, 2019). Jacques Derrida, speaking of the Western philosophical tradition, suggests that while rhythm has never been central to its concerns, it has nonetheless haunted it (1989: 33). In his 1936 work *The Dialectic of Duration,* Gaston Bachelard titled chapter 8 "Rhythmanalysis". He highlights how this chapter refers to and draws directly on and is inspired by the 1931 work *Ritmanálise* by Lúcio Alberto Pinheiro dos Santos. Unfortunately, this original work remains untraceable. It is in *Ritmanálise* and then in Bachelard's 1936 development that we have the first (to our knowledge) usages of the term *rhythmanalysis.* Bachelard sought to highlight the fruitfulness of the rhythmanalytical approach (2016: 123), but it was not until 1992 that Lefebvre's *Rhythmanalysis* would be published (the year after his death). Lefebvre's text has, to date, proved most influential, and it functions as a *de facto* fourth volume of his three-volume *Critique of Everyday Life.* The question of rhythm is present and scattered at different points in the official three volumes, becoming centrally thematised in the unofficial fourth. Lefebvre's *Rhythmanalysis* also included collaborative studies with Catherine Régulier. Translated into English in 2004 by Stuart Elden and Gerald Moore, Lefebvre's *Rhythmanalysis* has gained the most attention from the fields of geography and social sciences. The 2004 collection *Reanimating Places: A Geography of Rhythm* edited by Tom Mels (2016) as well as the 2010 collection *Geographies of Rhythm* edited by Tim Edensor (2016) are both key in this regard. Works by Michel Alhadeff-Jones (2017) on rhythm and education as well as two more recent methodological texts by Yi Chen (2018) and Dawn Lyon (2019) all offer novel and practical ways of deploying rhythmanalysis and provide frameworks for other researchers to develop. Although the author does not directly draw on the notion of *rhythmanalysis* as a starting point, it is also vital to mention Pascal Michon's (2018a, 2018b, 2019, 2021a, 2021b) multivolume work on "rhythmology", which traces the history of the notion in European thought and addresses Lefebvre in volume IV. It is essential to highlight that amongst these texts there is no one unified set of methodological steps giving any would-be rhythmanalysts a "how-to". Let us nonetheless highlight three common threads.

First, at the most general level, we of course find a mutual commitment to making rhythm a principle of analysis. The form this takes, as well as what different rhythm-objects are emphasised, varies. A central form this often takes is in what may be termed the *ontologisation* of rhythm. Two examples of such ontologisation are worth mentioning.

First, Bachelard, drawing on Pinheiro dos Santos's account of rhythms in *matter*, suggests that both matter and radiation 'must have wave and rhythmic characteristics' (2016: 124). Matter is treated as moving in different forms of undulation and at different frequencies. To subtract the rhythm (e.g., through treating matter as a *static* object) would be to subtract matter's dynamic processes and fail to adequately conceptualise it. Considering seemingly inert objects – such as a stone, a table, or Bachelard's example of the pyramids of Egypt – the rhythmanalyst understands each of these as themselves dynamic processes. The chair is built with 'an anarchy of vibrations' and the pyramids are 'endless cacophonies' (2016: 124). To exist is to *vibrate in time* or as *durative undulation:* 'If a particle ceased to vibrate, it would cease to be' (2016: 125). We have the theorisation of the movement of matter in time as forming a rhythmic materialism or vibrational ontology.

The second example is in Lefebvre who suggests that 'the act of rhythmanalysis integrates these things – this wall, this table, these trees – in a dramatic becoming, in an ensemble full of meaning, transforming them no longer into diverse things, but into presences' (2013: 33). Rhythmanalysis is for Lefebvre a type of embodied engagement with the processes that we are directed towards and enmeshed within. Both the rhythmanalyst and the rhythm-objects are in motion and process. *Observation* of objects already is a form of (aesthetic) participation and cannot be considered in the manner of a neutral and static subject observing an inert and motionless object. Considering the example of music, ethnomusicologist Thomas Turino describes music as *semiotically dense*, referring to the fact that engaging with music recruits multiple senses simultaneously 'since vocal tone, rhythm, inflection, and physical and facial gestures add a whole range of additional signs occurring simultaneously with the words' (2008: 108). The rhythmanalyst extends this recognition of music's semiotic density to the social field, noting that such aesthetic and semiotic density captures our experience of everyday life. To repeat something we mentioned in the Introduction: the realms of art are *particular* realms of aesthetic experimentation, but our milieus are entirely aesthetic. Think again of the aesthetic, semiotic, and performative density of the criminal trial, a ritual procedure with ordered, sequenced movements which enlists the participation and synchronised performance of those within it. Such aesthetic density and enlistment of participation are perhaps particularly emphasised in the trial, but are no less present in everyday life, just operating at a different rhythmic modality; Yi Chen has, for example, conducted a rhythmanalytical study (2018: 73–110) of bodily rhythms when walking in London's East End, describing how the biorhythmic is experienced in relation to London's dense aesthetic, semiotic, and performative technorhythmic field. For Lefebvre, this way of thinking has important methodological implications, as the rhythmanalyst 'thinks with his [sic] body, not in the abstract, but in lived temporality' (2013: 31, our addition).

In these respects, it is fair to associate rhythmanalysis with the broader terrain of what is known as *process philosophy*. Process philosophy is a field which situates itself against classical "substance metaphysics" in two broad senses. First, substance metaphysics has an idea of "being" as fundamentally static and unchangeable. Second, and similarly, substance metaphysics will tend to presuppose the unity, stability, and substantiality of the subject. For process philosophy, as with rhythmanalysis as discussed in the previous paragraph, being and all objects are better thought of in a continuous activity of becoming and, likewise the subject is itself is engaged in a continuous activity of becoming. Whitehead, a contemporary of both Pinheiro dos Santos and Bachelard, is considered one of the key figures in the formulation of process philosophy, particularly in his 1929 work *Process and Reality:*

An Essay in Cosmology. Whitehead often uses rhythm as a fundamental category in his philosophy of organism, but he also explores it in other contexts (Heaney, 2020). For example, in his 1925 work *Principles of Natural Knowledge,* Whitehead accords to rhythm the sign of vital activity: 'Life is the rhythm as such . . . wherever there is some rhythm, there is some life' (2017: 197). In *Process in Reality,* he states:

> The atom is only explicable as a society with activities involving rhythms with their definite periods . . . quanta of energy are associated by a simple law with the periodic rhythms which we detect in the molecules. Thus the quanta are, themselves, in their own nature, somehow vibratory; but they emanate from the protons and electrons. Thus there is every reason to believe that rhythmic periods cannot be dissociated from the protonic and electronic entities.
>
> (1985: 78–79)

Rhythmanalysis may proceed, therefore, through making rhythm a foundational principle in theorising existence from a broadly processual standpoint. This idea is not universally shared amongst rhythmanalysts, however, and more empirically focused research may instead zoom in on particular rhythm-objects for empirical study rather than explicitly focusing on such ontological questions. Our approach is to try to move between these abstract and concrete emphases.

Considering the second common thread, rhythmanalysis will tend to centralise temporality and its aesthetic embodiment. This focus on embodiment puts all rhythmanalyses in touch with everyday life, and in particular on the relationship between the biorhythmic, cosmorhythmic, and the technosocial rhythmic. Rhythmanalysis enlists the body, not just the mind. Yi Chen approaches rhythm as a "meta-sense", encompassing the entire ambient aesthetic atmosphere; rhythm is not simply about sound, sight, smell, touch, and other senses, but about the 'differential relations of the senses' (2018: 3). This dynamic relationship between the biorhythmic, cosmorhythmic, and technosocial rhythmic is central in particular to the distinction made by Lefebvre and Régulier between *linear* and *cyclical* time. Linear time, the central case of which is clock time, is positioned as abstract, quantitative, and homogeneous, imposing 'monotonous repetitions' (2013: 83) and fragmenting time into slices. Biorhythmic and cosmorhythmic cycles constitute the main examples of cyclical time; the repetitions of cyclical rhythms are described as invigorating, with the sense given that there is replenishment and renewal accomplished through biorhythmic and cosmorhythmic cycles. Technosocial rhythms, on the other hand, are the central examples of linear time: labour is extracted from workers on the basis that their labour is measured and remunerated on the basis of time-measurement. Time moves forwards. The repetitions of linear time consist in a 'series of identical facts separated by long or short periods of time' (2013: 85): the working day and the repetitions of working procedures, break time, overtime, the weekend, and so forth. As Warren D. TenHouten notes,

> Clock time, by linking labor power and machines, created the standardized, metronomic rhythms of industrial work. . . . Linear, clock time reaches its fullest expression in the urbanized, northern countries of seventeenth-century Europe as they developed competitive, capitalistic economics.
>
> (2005: 172)

Lefebvre and Régulier, as well as approaches drawing on their work, will therefore tend to emphasise in their rhythmanalytical approaches the ways in which the *cyclical* and *linear* interact in everyday life and most particularly in the body. The cyclical and the linear are locked, for Lefebvre and Régulier, in a 'bitter and dark struggle around time and the use of time' (2015: 83) forming an 'antagonistic unity' (2013: 85). It is not simply the case of "natural" time being placed on one side of a binary and "cultural" or "social" time as the other side, but more about their combined complex interactions and effects on everyday life.

Third, rhythmanalyses will tend to develop some sort of *typology* of rhythm. By a typology of rhythm, we mean that the rhythmanalyst, when faced with the range and scope of natural, technical, social, and other processes, will seek to offer some way of distinguishing between different rhythms, providing certain *criteria of judgment*, a reasoned *measure* for analytical distinction and adjudication. The development of typologies in this way will therefore be closely tied to, at the very least, some sort of *normative* gesture. For example, a common distinction made here is between the *eurhythmic* (the prefix "eu" denoting "good") and the *arrhythmic* (the prefix "a" denoting "not, without"). Lefebvre (2013: 30) describes the eurhythmic body as harmonious and healthy, and he theorises arrhythmia in terms of a disruption or disturbance that risks becoming pathological. Aristotle uses this distinction to clarify the difference between certain sentence formations (Vatri, 2020: 476–477). Rudolf Laban distinguishes between eurhythmy and kakorhythmy (a term he uses to refer to patterns whose structure is not perceived as symmetrical or proportional), imagining the potential of art, education, and festival to train us to experience and embody the eurhythmic, which in his formulation is framed as type of connection to the flow of all things, the 'all-encompassing rhythm [Allrhythmus]' (2014: 77). Émile Jaques-Dalcroze's famous musical pedagogy is simply called *eurhythmics*. As Andrea Mubi Brighenti and Mattias Kärrholm (2018) suggest, the prefixes (*eu-* and *a-*) are 'always correlative to a judgment, to an evaluative point of view'. What constitutes the *eurhythmic* for Plato will not at all be the same as what it will be for Lefebvre. The making of these typologies is therefore a *task* for the would-be rhythmanalyst.

§5.2 Recent Rhythmanalyses

Given its transdisciplinary reach, it is perhaps not surprising that rhythmanalysis ought maybe to be considered less as a single methodology and more as a plural and open methodological field. The proper analytical tools need to be developed in relation to the specifics of the research: someone interested in working on metaphysical questions will need to develop their own questions and adjust the methodological techniques appropriately, as will the sociologist, the geographer, the legal researcher, and so on. Rhythmanalysis provides the starting point as well as a set of foci, and it provides the student of rhythm with a range of examples of its power and concrete connection to our everyday lives. It is, however, still appropriate and useful to broadly group together these different styles of approach under the title *rhythmanalysis*. Those interested exclusively, for example, in poetic rhythm or biological rhythm cannot be said to be doing *rhythmanalysis* in the sense we are using it, insofar as such research does not necessarily link up with those three common threads. Such research is focused on specific rhythm-objects, not on rhythm as a principle. But this does not at all mean that such work cannot be mobilised rhythmanalytically. Through making rhythm a principle, the rhythmanalyst treats *all* objects as rhythm-objects, potentially bringing into their analytical purview all these different fields of study.

Let us now consider some recent work in rhythmanalysis. We will take three examples, each of which has approached distinct *markets* with the tools of rhythmanalysis, allowing us to evidence further aspects of the three common threads as well as the versatility of rhythmanalysis given how it can be creatively approached depending on the context and aims of the research, as well as the critical and political significance of these styles.

First, Christian Borch, Kristian Bondo Hansen, and Ann-Christina Lange conducted a comparative rhythmanalysis of two distinct financial market trading contexts. On the one hand was the "open–outcry pit". This is the "classic" image of the trading floor, characterised by its octagonal or round shape, the close proximity of traders, intensity, speed, and the volume which is so loud that communication must take place either via shouting or hand signals. In the open outcry pit, the body is present as the central instrument of trading: the market mobilises multiple senses, and trading is effectuated through the gestures and movements of bodies. The call to financial trading is marked by the gong which opens proceedings. This centralisation of bodily participation in the market accords with the rhythmanalyst's central concern with the aesthetics and temporality of the market context. Pit traders seek 'the state of eurhythmia, i.e. a harmonious unity of rhythms of body and market' (Borch et al., 2015: 1087). Markets have the potential to become atmospheres of affective and emotional contagion where each trader's movements and decisions beat to the rhythm of the market.

The second financial market trading context they consider is the high-frequency trade (HFT) markets that developed towards the end of the 20th century and the gradual transition to their dominance (Lyon, 2019: 61; Rooney, 2021: 75) which forms a case in point of the more general technorhythmic transition towards digitalisation. Trading is increasingly computerised and necessarily facilitated upon the management and supervision of trading algorithms. Traders do not seek the same state of eurhythmia as in the open–outcry pit, they instead 'calibrate their bodily rhythms to their algorithms' (Borch et al., 2015: 1091). Such a calibration is biorhythmically challenging in a similar sense to the challenges of shift work we mentioned previously. The communication of HFT information is rapid. Using microwave technology, 'the current roundtrip time for data transmission between Chicago and New York (the most important route in US financial markets) is about 8.1 milliseconds. By comparison, a blink of an eye takes 3–400 milliseconds' (Borch et al., 2015: 1092). To be calibrated to the algorithm comes at a biorhythmic cost. The shifts towards more abstract linearised forms of time-measurement and their institution through the development of capitalist economies and modern science demanded that work (in whatever form) synchronises to the clock. The techno-rhythmic transition towards digitalisation means that it is increasingly about the calibration of our bodies and attention to the algorithm, as with the high-frequency trader.

Second, Emily Reid-Musson's recent work has critiqued and developed Lefebvre by forwarding an *intersectional* rhythmanalysis. While Lefebvre centralises the body, he plays little attention to the multiple ways in which embodiment differentially attunes our everyday rhythms. Building on this, Reid-Musson works with aspects of Kimberlé Crenshaw's foundational work on intersectionality (1989, 1991) and Ruth Wilson Gilmore's work on the *fatal* couplings of power and difference in racism (Gilmore, 2002; also see Hall, 1992: 17). Reid-Musson seeks to develop an approach to rhythmanalysis appropriate to critical scholarship interested in the experience and manifestation of inequalities and differential power structures in everyday life. Her research focused on migrant farmworkers employed through Canada's Seasonal Agricultural Worker Program (SAWP), through which farm employers seasonally hire workers from Mexico and the English-speaking Caribbean. This work is tied to economic cycles themselves tied to agricultural rhythms, and workers are regulated according to a strict regime regulating spatial and temporal freedom, with deportation featuring as a 'disciplinary tool to ensure worker compliance' (Reid-Musson, 2018: 889; Basok et al., 2013). In such a regime, migrant workers are essential but do not have access to the temporal right to permanency or citizenship status. As well as highlighting the differential gendered distribution of the migrant workforces and their different regimes (with women facing more severe restrictions), Reid-Musson (2018: 893) offers a rhythmanalysis of the ways in which the SAWP 'tightly organizes and manages migrants' daily, weekly, and seasonal rhythms', highlighting the 'racial, colonial, gender, and sexual politics to rhythms and the differential and deeply illiberal interventions operating at the level of rhythms'.

Finally, Dawn Lyon (2019: 67–72) has researched the alternative timescape of London's Billingsgate fish market, a marketplace which officially starts at 4:00 am but which unofficially begins around 1:00 am, operating as an integral preliminary beat in the food supply chain of the day. With a rhythmanalytical orientation, Lyon documented the fish market through her embodied engagement, time-lapse photography, and sound (in collaboration with Kevin Reynolds). As she notes, the technical use of time-lapse photography allowed an almost panoptic view of the kinetic and sonic energies exchanged in the dynamics of the fish market which become obscured whenever one is fully immersed in the market itself. This full immersion can be an aesthetic overload, just as with the atmosphere and emotional contagion of the open-outcry pits. In these pits, certain traders regulated themselves against such contagion through the application of techniques of recording (such as using a pencil and pad to record movements), discern potential contagion, then betting *against* the tendencies of the market in a tradition known as *contrarian speculation* (Borch et al., 2015: 1089). This technique enabled the trader to not be fully immersed or synchronised with the potentially misleading animal spirits of the market, in order for them to practice a different rhythm of financial speculation. Contrarian speculators thereby sought a balance between 'observation and participation, i.e. being able to detect the psychological rhythms of the market without having their own psyche contaminated by the market crowd's purportedly irrational behavior' (Borch et al., 2015: 1089). Lyon indicates her reasons for deploying time-lapse photography to aid in the rhythmanalytical documentation of Bilingsgate so as to capture the temporality of the market from a different vantage point, in a way not possible through the body due to the 'sensory excess of the market space' (Lyon, 2019: 68). The deployment of (audiovisual) technological recording functioned to multiply the perspectives through which to analyse market rhythms (see Simpson, 2012).

Lefebvre discussed this balancing act of the rhythmanalyst (where the body is an important instrument of analysis, but an instrument which risks being too affectively immersed) in terms of having, on the one hand, a certain *exteriority* to the rhythm in question ('be it through illness or a technique' [2013: 37]) to make some abstract analysis possible, and on the other, a certain *interiority* whereby the rhythmanalyst can still be to some extent *grasped* (2013: 37) by the rhythm. Illness allows us to have a certain exteriority with respect to our predominant biorhythms. The contrarian speculator seeks this balance through the to and fro between participation in the market along with techniques of recording (pencil and pad). Lyon's balance was primarily through visual ethnography. Lefebvre thinks that the view from the *balcony* of a city street is an ideal vantage point, and his study of urban Parisian rhythms is a key case study in attempting this rhythmanalytical balancing act. Rhythmanalysts must not be too close, but also not too far, from that which they analyse. The upshot here is that even though we do not have a precise formulation on how one might achieve this balance between being "inside" and "outside" the phenomena we study, it is a vital methodological consideration for the rhythmanalyst. One's body is an indispensable condition for research, and one of the key strengths of the rhythmanalytical approach is precisely this grounding of research in the lived body engaged in everyday life which, after all, is the only place research happens. This area between being totally immersed and totally detached from our object of study can be a grey one, but this only enhances the importance that it is methodologically considered and scrutinised. The rhythmanalyst is as such dismissive of the notion of a disinterested spectator or researcher who neutrally executes methodological rules as a functional bureaucrat of knowledge-production. Rather, rhythmanalysts work from the only place they can, in the *middle*, in between, or moving back and forth between the abstract and concrete (or the subject and the object, or the ideal and material). Gilles Deleuze (1988: 123) captures this: 'One never commences; one never has a *tabula rasa*; one slips in, enters in the middle; one takes up or lays down rhythms'.

This condensed discussion of a few different recent rhythmanalyses has been designed to offer a snapshot of how the rhythmanalytical orientation shares methodological orientations and concerns, but it can be creatively developed and innovated. Of critical and political significance, these approaches allowed rhythmic differentiation to be discerned between different market contexts, as well as critical attention to be paid to the ways in which we can become affectively overwhelmed in semiotically dense atmospheres, and the differential distribution of rhythms for workers.

§6 The Nomorhythmic Object

Looping back to a point we made in §3 (drawing on Miller), we note that milieus reproduce (and transform) themselves through the *sampling* of social practices, such as through tradition, custom, and ritual. Sampling, it was noted, is both a technique of *repetition* (binding it to the past) but also of *creation* (each sample is always *this* sample, recontextualising what has passed and what is to come). The example of democratic practices there discussed is one indebted to Graeme Orr, whose book *Ritual and Rhythm in Electoral Systems* will be the basis of this concluding section as we draw on his research as a rare case where the rhythm-law nexus has been taken seriously.

Orr does not explicitly draw on rhythmanalysis, and often his treatment of rhythm subsumes it *within* the more central concept of ritual or as denoting primarily *repetition*. Ritual is preliminarily approached as involving a collective participating symbolically in some practice, adding to this 'the need for ritual to be rhythmic, or at least be capable of repetition' (2015: 14). Orr is explicit in identifying and analysing *elections* as (to use our terminology) nomorhythmic objects:

> Elections are nothing if not rhythmical. They have a rhythm whether taken holistically as recurrent events, or whether looked at in terms of their internal timetable, which unfolds from the first appearance of potential candidate, through the process of voting and election night and onto the swearing-in of successful candidates.
>
> (2015: 14)

We have highlighted already that *both* repetition and difference are entangled in the concept of rhythm. We can now add a third element through the example of elections. As Lefebvre notes, 'Everywhere there is rhythm, there is *measure*, which is to say law, calculated and expected obligation, a project' (2013: 18). The French term *la mesure* has multiple senses relevant to music and law: length measurement, temporal measurement (beat and tempo), acting with *moderation*, and *taking measures* for certain purposes (regulations, rules). In rhythm's temporal unfolding, it will incorporate particular measures and judgments. *Elections* themselves are the formation of collective judgments, and these judgments organise the next *measured beat* in the rhythm of the electoral cycle in both *form* (in the sense that each successful election legitimates the entire formal process of that particular electoral cycle) and *content* (in the sense that each election constitutes a collective judgment which reshuffles the co-ordinates of political power and impacts upon the milieu's movement into the future).

Orr defines his approach to elections within a *non-instrumental* approach to law. Conventional approaches to elections are generally instrumentalist, that is, their focus is on achieving certain aims or goals. Orr contrasts two (2015: 6–7): first, the 'structural integrity' (or 'competitive') model, which understands elections as primarily about ensuring some appropriate level of electoral competition; second, the 'liberal rights' model, which understands elections primarily as about civil liberty to participate in the democratic process (however thinly or thickly we cash out the term "participate"). This is a not a distinction of mutual exclusivity, and Orr offers some methodological notes which chime with the rhythmanalyst. First, elections are the subject of embodied experience and symbolic practice. Second, elections are indissociable from their temporality, whether we think about this in terms of how each election cycle broadly repeats the previous cycle, functioning to promote a sense of (and potentially aid in the constitution of) political renewal and replenishment, or in terms of the bureaucratic regulation of election timetables. The right to vote is itself a rite of passage which is usually purely a marker of temporality (such as turning 18). Third, Orr also highlights the recursive relationship between law and elections: on the one hand, elections are constructs of law, regulated and officiated by rules, customs, and conventions; and on the other, law is a product of elections, since elections provide the grounds upon which subsequent legislative activity is legitimated. The two oscillate in a recursive loop. Orr's call is for us to understand elections aesthetically and temporally through a non-instrumental approach to elections and electoral law, where this emphasis on the rhythmic and ritualistic dimensions of elections is leveraged to underline that elections 'are not means to ends so much as ends in themselves' (2015: 8). Orr does not undermine the clear instrumental purposes of elections, but rather asks us to pay attention to the ways that the scheduled theatricality and collective performance of elections is about more than simply achieving electoral results, and that we ought to pay attention to their qualitative, experiential, and temporal elements as well as their more often emphasised quantitative and arithmetic ones.

Admittedly, sometimes the election may simply be a rubber-stamp process veering more towards a simple repetition of existing power relations, as with electoral processes in North Korea returning 99 per cent turnout and 100 per cent support for unchallenged Party-approved candidates. Sometimes the election process may allow for slightly more collective agency over how the milieu in question moves into the future, but it could still face the criticism of broadly reproducing permanent oligarchic governance, as might often be said for countries such as America and the UK (2015: 19). These social rhythms and rituals may be more or less empty of substantive content and function more to produce the *feeling* that we are participating in a democratic process (as a symbolic substitution for substantive democracy). Notwithstanding, any imagined "fully realised" and "authentic" democratic process would realise it *through* ritual and rhythm in participatory forms.

Electoral cycles are technosocial rhythms which co-ordinate collective judgment in the rhythm of political power, structuring a central social ritual which provides periodic replenishment of juridico-political legitimacy as much as it can be a ritual of purgation where an electorate dissociates itself from the previous cycle. Orr even parallels electoral cycles with cosmorhythms (2015: 31): 'Just as fundamental physical laws determine the orbit of a satellite or comet, so the electoral cycle is determined by core facts of constitutional law'. In certain circumstances, electoral cycles can produce unexpected results, shifting the direction the milieu takes as it moves into the future. Further still, there are more in-depth questions about how, for example, to think about electoral cycles in longer-term frameworks (Elazar, 1978; Fischer, 1996) or the shifting patterns of collaboration or defiance between different branches of government (Lindsay, 2003).

We noted in §3 key dimensions of *nomos*, that is, distributive, behavioural, and regulatory. Treating elections as *nomorhythmic* objects allows us to explore the rhythm-law nexus across these dimensions. Access to or control over the *distributive* dimension of law is one of the key elements at stake in elections themselves, providing as it does access to the privilege of lawmaking, policy, and resource distribution. With regard to the *behavioural* and *regulatory* dimensions, Orr mentions how law can sometimes directly determine ritual (e.g., prescribed legal procedures) or open the space for new rituals in the electoral cycle. Taking the example of papal elections, there are practices which are strictly regulated to ensure secrecy, but elements of this election are continually evolving. The famous white smoke signalling a successful election is quite recent (probably from the 18th century) given papal elections have taken place in some way for nearly two thousand years. The preferred method for centuries was a cannon blast (2015: 24). Orr highlights how law can *impose* upon ritual experience, considering voter ID laws as an example where the rite of voting can become bureaucratically overloaded. In addition, voter ID laws can be exclusionary and disenfranchise multiple minority groups (Sobel and Smith, 2009; Hajnal et al., 2017). The right to vote involves a level of symbolic recognition of that citizen by the political community (Orr, 2015: 68), and participation in the rite of voting not only implies a level of symbolic recognition by that citizen of the political community, but also represents a ritual practice through which each voter *participates* in the perpetuation of the *nomorhythms* of elections themselves.

Orr mobilises this analysis to make some general practical and normative reflections. To take one example, he uses the image of elections as ritual events important in the replenishment of political vitality to express scepticism at moves towards more convenient forms of voting (e.g., postal voting or e-voting), in part because convenience voting can dilute the participatory ritual political replenishment that elections can offer. Instead, he suggests polling weekends or election holidays and the minimisation of queues, leaning towards treating elections as a form of secular rites (2015: 63–65). Orr's work constitutes an important contribution to the minimal work done on the rhythm-law nexus, underscoring its epistemological purchase in understanding the function and purpose of elections beyond mere instrumental reasons, as well as offering normative proposals.

§7 Conclusion

The purpose of this chapter has been to condense an immense transdisciplinary field to make the case that rhythm needs to be taken more seriously as both an object and principle of analysis. Rhythmanalysis is a field which treats all "objects" of analysis as rhythm-objects, and it can be understood as a type of *process philosophy* which treats the flux and flow of things as fundamental. Insofar as process is fundamental, we need an analytical approach which is capable of in-depth consideration of each, but also of conducting multi-level analysis. The cosmorhythmic, biorhythmic, and technosocial rhythmic (within which we discussed nomorhythms) are in continuous interaction, but it is important not to reduce one to the other. Our bodies have evolved in relation to cosmological movements, but this does not mean cosmorhythmic analysis precludes knowledge of biology. Biological factors play an important role in our individual development and life trajectories, but this does not mean biorhythmic analysis precludes knowledge of the technical and social environment. Rhythmanalysis offers an approach hugely underexplored and ripe for critical and creative exploration which can be sensitive across these levels.

References

Alhadeff-Jones, M. 2017. *Time and the Rhythms of Emancipatory Education: Rethinking the Temporal Complexity of Self and Society*. London: Routledge.
Bachelard, G. 2016. *The Dialectic of Duration*. Trans. M. McAllester Jones. London: Rowman & Littlefield International.

Baron, K. G. and Reid, K. J. 2014. Circadian Misalignment and Health. *International Review of Psychiatry*, 26(2): 139–154.

Basok, T., Bélanger, D. and Rivas, E. 2013. Reproducing Deportability: Migrant Agricultural Workers in South-western Ontario. *Journal of Ethnic and Migration Studies*, 40(9): 1394–1413.

Borch, C., Bondo Hansen, K. and Lange, A.-C. 2015. Markets, Bodies, and Rhythms: A Rhythmanalysis of Financial Markets from Open-outcry Trading to High-frequency Trading. *Environment and Planning D: Society and Space*, 33(6): 1080–1097.

Brighenti, A. M. and Kärrholm, M. 2018. Beyond Rhythmanalysis: Towards a Territoriology of Rhythms and Melodies in Everyday Spatial Activities. *City, Territory and Architecture*, 5(4).

Buhr, E. D., Yoo, S-H., and Takahashi, J. S. 2010. Temperature as a Universal Resetting Cue for Mammalian Circadian Oscillators. *Science*, 330(6002): 379–385.

Chen, Y. 2018. *Practising Rhythmanalysis: Theories and Methodologies*. London: Rowman & Littlefield.

Crenshaw, K. 1989. Demarginalizing the Intersection of Race and Sex: A Black Feminist Critique of Antidiscrimination Doctrine, Feminist Theory and Antiracist Politics. *University of Chicago Legal Forum*, 1(8): 139–167.

Crenshaw, K. 1991. Mapping the Margins: Intersectionality, Identity Politics, and Violence Against Women of Color. *Stanford Law Review*, 43(6): 1241–1299.

Czeisler, C.A., Duffy, J. F., Shanahan, T. L., Brown, E. N., Mitchell, J. F., Rimmer, D. W., Ronda, J. M., Silva, E. J., Allan, J. S., Emens, J. S., Dijk, D-J. and Kronauer, R. E. 1999. Stability, Precision, and Near-24-Hour Period of the Human Circadian Pacemaker. *Science*, 284: 2177–2181.

Deleuze, G. 1988. *Spinoza: Practical Philosophy*. Trans. R. Hurley. San Francisco, CA: City Lights Books.

Derrida, J. 1989. Introduction: Desistance. In *Typography: Mimesis, Philosophy, Politics*. Eds. P. Lacoue-Labarthe and C. Fynsk. Cambridge, MA: Harvard University Press, pp. 1–42.

Edensor, T. (Ed.). 2016. *Geographies of Rhythm: Nature, Place, Mobilities and Bodies*. London: Routledge.

Edwards, P. N. 2003. Infrastructure and Modernity: Force, Time, and Social Organization in the History of Sociotechnical Systems. In *Modernity and Technology*. Eds. T. J. Misa, P. Brey and A. Feenberg. Cambridge, MA: MIT Press, pp. 186–225.

Elazar, D. 1978. The Generational Rhythm of American Politics. *American Politics Quarterly*, 6(1): 55–94.

Fischer, D. H. 1996. *Price Revolutions and the Rhythm of History*. Oxford: Oxford University Press.

Fleming, T. J. 1977. The Musical Nomos in Aeschylus' Oresteia. *The Classical Journal*, 72(3): 222–233.

Gentry, N. W., Ashbrook, L. H., Fu, Y.-H. and Ptáček, L. J. 2021. Human Circadian Variations. *The Journal of Clinical Investigation*, 131(16): e148282.

Germain, A. and Kupfer, D. J. 2008. Circadian Rhythm Disturbances in Depression. *Human Psychopharmacology: Clinical and Experimental*, 23: 571–585.

Gilmore, R. W. 2002. Fatal Couplings of Power and Difference: Notes on Racism and Geography. *The Professional Geographer*, 54(1): 15–24.

Goodwin, B. 1996. Biology Is Just a Dance. In *The Third Culture*. Ed. J. Brockman. New York: Touchstone, pp. 96–110.

Hajnal, Z., Lajevardi, N. and Nielson, L. 2017. Voter Identification Laws and the Suppression of Minority Votes. *The Journal of Politics*, 79(2): 363–379.

Hall, S. 1992. Race, Culture, and Communications: Looking Backward and Forward at Cultural Studies. *Rethinking Marxism*, 5(1): 10–18.

Harvey, A. G. 2011. Sleep and Circadian Functioning: Critical Mechanisms in the Mood Disorders? *Annual Review of Clinical Psychology*, 7: 297–319.

Heaney, C. 2019. Tragic Rhythms: Nietzsche and Agamben on Rhythm and Art. *La Deleuziana*, 10: 61–78.

Heaney, C. 2020. Rhythmic Nootechnics: Stiegler, Whitehead, and Noetic Life. *Educational Philosophy and Theory*, 52(4): 397–408.

Ikoniadou, E. 2012. A Rhythmic Time for the Digital. *The Senses and Society*, 7(3): 261–275.

Ikoniadou, E. 2014. *The Rhythmic Event: Art, Media, and the Sonic*. Cambridge, MA: MIT Press.

Jalas, M., Rinkinen, J. and Silvast, A. 2016. The Rhythms of Infrastructure. *Anthropology Today*, 32(4): 17–20.

Kelly, T. L., Neri, D. F., Grill, J. T., Ryman, D., Hunt, P. D., Dijk, D-J, Shanahan, T. L. and Czeisler. C. A. 1999. Nonentrained Circadian Rhythms of Melatonin in Submariners Scheduled to an 18-Hour Day. *Journal of Biological Rhythms*, 14(3): 190–196.

Laban, R. 2014. Eurhythmy and Kakorhythmy in Art and Education. Trans. P. Crespi. *Body & Society*, 20(3–4): 75–78.

Lefebvre, H. 2013. *Rhythmanalysis: Space, Time and Everyday Life*. Trans. S. Elden and G. Moore. London: Bloomsbury Academic.

Liddell, H. G. and Scott, R. 2017. *Liddell and Scott's Greek-English Lexicon Abridged*. London: Simon Wallenberg Press.

Lindsay, J. M. 2003. Deference and Defiance: The Shifting Rhythms of Executive-Legislative Relations in Foreign Policy. *Presidential Studies Quarterly*, 33(3): 530–546.

Lyon, D. 2019. *What Is Rhythmanalysis?* London: Bloomsbury Academic.

Mels, T. (Ed.). 2016. *Reanimating Places: A Geography of Rhythm*. Oxon: Routledge.

Michon, P. 2018a. *Elements of Rhythmology: I. Antiquity*. Paris: Rhuthmos.

Michon, P. 2018b. *Elements of Rhythmology: II. From the Renaissance to the 19th Century*. Paris: Rhuthmos.

Michon, P. 2019. *Elements of Rhythmology: III. The Spread of Metron from the 1840s to the 1910s*. Paris: Rhuthmos.

Michon, P. 2021a. *Elements of Rhythmology: IV. A Rhythmic Constellation – the 1970s*. Paris: Rhuthmos.

Michon, P. 2021b. *Elements of Rhythmology: V. A Rhythmic Constellation – the 1980s*. Paris: Rhuthmos.

Miller, P. D. 2004. *Rhythm Science*. Cambridge, MA: MIT Press.

Moore, G. D. 2017. On the Origin of Aisthesis by Means of Artificial Selection; or, The Preservation of Favored Traces in the Struggle for Existence. *Boundary 2*, 44(1): 191–212.

Orr, G. 2015. *Ritual and Rhythm in Electoral Systems: A Comparative Legal Account*. Surrey: Ashgate.

Refinetti, R. and Menaker, M. 1992. The Circadian Rhythm of Body Temperature. *Physiology & Behavior*, 51: 613–637.

Reid-Musson, E. 2018. Intersectional Rhythmanalysis: Power, Rhythm, and Everyday Life. *Progress in Human Geography*, 42(6): 881–897.

Scheer, F. A. J. L., Wright Jr., K. P., Kronauer, R. E. Czeisler, C. A. 2007. Plasticity of the Intrinsic Period of the Human Circadian Timing System. *PLoS One*, 2(8): e721.

Scofield, B. 2011. Cosmic Rhythms of Life. In *Chimeras and Consciousness: Evolution of the Sensory Self*. Eds. L. Margulis, C. A. Asikainen and W. E. Krumbein. London: The MIT Press, pp. 109–121.

Siffre, M. 1975. Six Months Alone in a Cave. *National Geographic*, 147(3): 426–435.

Simpson, P. 2012. Apprehending Everyday Rhythms: Rhythmanalysis, Time-lapse Photography, and the Space-times of Street Performance. *Cultural Geographies*, 19(4): 423–445.

Sobel, R. and Smith, R. E. 2009. Voter-ID Laws Discourage Participation, Particularly among Minorities, and Trigger a Constitutional Remedy in Lost Representation. *Political Science and Politics*, 42(1): 107–110.

Stiegler, B. 2009. *Technics and Time, 2: Disorientation*. Trans. S. Barker. Stanford, CA: Stanford University Press.

TenHouten, W. D. 2005. *Time and Society*. Albany, NY: State University of New York Press.

Turino, T. 2008. *Music as Social Life: The Politics of Participation*. Chicago, IL: University of Chicago Press.

Vatri, A. 2020. The Nature and Perception of Attic Prose Rhythm. *Classical Philology*, 115: 467–485.

Whitehead, A. N. 1967. *The Aims of Education and Other Essays*. New York: The Free Press.

Whitehead, A. N. 1985. *Process and Reality: An Essay in Cosmology*. New York: The Free Press.

Whitehead, A. N. 2017. *An Enquiry Concerning the Principles of Natural Knowledge*. Eastford, CT: Martino Fine Books.

2

Cosmological and Nomological Order

§8 Yet Another Footnote to Plato

The rhythm-law nexus with which this book is concerned is one which was foreseen and addressed by Plato – as is the case with so many philosophical problems. In this chapter, we will explicate this by examining Plato's later work on the theorisation of law, including how Plato situated law within a *cosmological* framework and the role rhythm plays in connecting *cosmos* with *nomos*. As well as providing a comparative context evidencing how rhythm can be deployed in thinking about law, this will also allow us to explore the rich history of our central concept. The first key aim of this chapter is to provide this context, adding historical precedent to our own study.

We will first survey the etymological discussions surrounding rhythm, tracing it from the earliest available evidence of its usage in Ancient Greek. By the time it reaches Plato, there is already a significant inheritance, and Plato made some contributions to how the term was used in a way which would prove historically significant, insofar as it still shapes much of our thinking about the term (§9). Plato, of course, was part of his own juridico-political context, but it is from this period that rhythm becomes more firmly associated with the proper *ordering of movements*. For Plato, the ordered movements of the heavenly bodies are the exemplar of *order* itself available in the visible world. This exemplary status ought to be taken very seriously, not just when seeking knowledge of the natural world, but in the design of our juridico-political institutions and as a model for everyday conduct. In §10, we will consider Plato's cosmology in the *Timaeus*, as it forms an important background for the *Laws* (considered in §11). There is no dialogue where Plato addresses rhythm more than in the *Laws*. The lawmaker is like a rhythmic governor, conducting the movements and speech of

2

DOI: 10.4324/9781003350231-3

citizens in the juridico-political space in such a way that the *city-state* might imitate the motions of the heavens, achieving stability, harmony, and order thereby. The second key aim of this chapter is to contribute to the developing but still underexplored literature on the enduring richness of Plato's late dialogues for thinking about the intersections between cosmology, music, politics, and law.

In §12, the third and final key aim of the chapter will be focused on the pertinence of Plato's cosmologically informed juridico-political theory from our perspective of conducting a rhythmanalysis of law. We will argue that Plato offers an account of law which is at once cosmological, mathematical, and musical, and through which *cosmos* and *nomos* are bound together, each partaking in their own ways to the ordered motion of the visible world of becoming. It is not simply a descriptive theory of what the cosmos is or what law is, but rather it is as much a prescriptive theory through which Plato adduces normative arguments for how *we* ought to live and how we ought to organise our juridico-political organs so as to harmonise and beat appropriately to cosmic movements. Conceptualising society and citizenship as *musical* is not metaphoric. It draws attention to the *participatory* dimension of our co-production of social order, the *aesthetic* dimension of such order, as well as the *temporal* component governing social practices, rituals, traditions, and everyday life. The budding rhythmanalyst senses rich resources for thinking imaginatively and critically about our legal institutions and practices via Plato.

§9 Rhythm's Etymology and Platonic Rhythm

This section will not be able to do justice to the fruitfulness (and ambiguities) of the debates related to the concept of rhythm considered primarily through its ancient usages. Our primary purpose is to lay the groundwork for the later sections of this chapter. As such, we will first briefly survey elements of the etymology of rhythm; second, highlight pre-Platonic approaches; and finally, focus on the key distinctions and definitions brought by Plato.

Rhythm has developed as a term via Latin and Greek. Potential ambiguities immediately arise when we take the two central translations in Latin. It was common, as can be seen both in the work of Cicero and in St Augustine (Formarier, 2013; Meyer-Baer, 1953), for the term *numerus* to be used to convey rhythm. *Numerus*, however, can also mean *measure* and *number*. This seemingly direct connection between "rhythm", "measure", and "number", however, was not always the case.

The second term in Latin is the less-used *rhythmus*, which is a translit-eration from its Greek origins, to which we now turn.

The Greek root ῥυθμός (*ruthmós*; or ῥυσμός [*rusmós*] in Ionian) is documented from the first half of the 7th century BCE. We find its earliest usage (in the Ionic form) at the end of Archilochus's Frag-ment 67A when, at the end of poetic fragment, he exhorts us (and himself) to 'appreciate the rhythm that controls men's lives' (quoted in Gerber, 1999: 167), goading us to remain steadfast and balanced amidst the sorrows and joys of life wrought by the forces which form us. That rhythm that controls life is 'at once external and internal to humans', and while outside of our control, it can be responded to through the application of appreciation and ethico-affective mod-eration (Barletta, 2016: 49). Rhythm is that which constrains human action, but also that which can give it 'form and meaning' (Barletta, 2020: 3). Discussing this fragment, Werner Jaeger (1965: 126) links the use of rhythm here as pertaining to cosmic and natural cycles and as most probably linked to Ionian natural philosophy. Therefore, in this first usage of the term *rhythm*, we have an immediate connection to the cosmorhythmic.

With regard to the meaning and etymology of the term, Jaeger dis-putes the semantic connection between rhythm and *flow* (the prefix ῥέω, *rhéō*, to flow), instead emphasising the *holding* function of rhythm. Robert Renehan builds on Jaeger, further disputing the derivation from flow, and underlines the importance of holding or binding to rhythm, naming the original meaning as 'the manner in which a thing is held together' (1963: 37). Among the elements that must be empha-sised in these early usages of rhythm are the ways in which it is associ-ated with a force which *confines, holds, limits,* and *binds.* We can refer to this as the *binding* function of rhythm for brevity; the bind of rhythm is the establishment of temporal continuity or integrity, exhibiting *some* apparent level of persistence amidst change and flow. The rhythm of the breath, for example, is the way in which the breath is temporally continuous, but this does not mean that every breath is the same or even that the rhythm remains the same.

Central to the discussion surrounding rhythm's etymology remains the piece by Émile Benveniste, "The Notion of 'Rhythm' in its Lin-guistic Expression", originally published in 1951. Benveniste argues for the importance of a distinction in the development and use of ῥυθμός which he ascribes to Plato's interventions. While Archilo-chus's use of the term was poetic, the first technical and *philosophical* uses of the term are attributed to the ancient atomists Leucippus and

Democritus (Benveniste, 1971: 282). In Aristotle's explanation (2016: 11), Leucippus and Democritus identified the basic elements of onto-logical differentiation as being rhythm (form, shape, schema), contact (order), and position (turning). Benveniste underlines that for these ancient atomists, ῥυθμός was primarily related to *form, shape,* or *schema* and reliably referred to the distinctive and proportioned form, figure, or arrangement of things (1971: 285). However, given the multiple distinct words which could refer to *form* – such as *schema* (σχῆμα) which we already mentioned, but also morphḗ (μορφή) and eidos (εἶδος) – Benveniste here argues that ῥυθμός cannot simply be defined as form, if by form we are referring to some fixed or static object (1971: 285). Instead, the earlier uses of ῥυθμός must be understood as *fluid* form, as the contraction/stabilisation of a pattern in the context of at least *some* type of flow. That is, in addition to the *binding* function of rhythm (associating rhythm with form, shape, boundary, and limit), Benveniste points us towards the indissociably *processual* or *flowing* character of rhythm.

Unlike Jaeger and Renehan, Benveniste does not fully dissociate rhythm from the prefix ῥέω, finding the connection morphologically 'satisfying' (1971: 285), even if semantically wanting. It is semantically wanting, Benveniste argues, *if* we take this prefix to pertain to a flow in the sense of the regular movement of the waves, as it is not said that the sea *flows*. Rivers and streams flow, but the sea does not have rhythm (1971: 281–282). Instead, Benveniste claims that ῥυθμός can be understood through properly considering the role of the suffix θμός (-*thmós*). This suffix, Benveniste claims, pertains to the *aesthetic* (i.e., sensible) *modality* of the accomplishment of an act or pattern of movement (dancing, placing, or other patterns of movement) (1971: 285). *Rhythm* is form as a particular patterned contraction in the context of sensible flows, designating 'the form in the instant that it is assumed by what is moving, mobile and fluid' (1971: 285–286): rhythm as bounded flow or as aesthetic modality of flux. By retaining an adjusted association with the prefix ῥέω, Benveniste notes that this prefix signified the *essential predication* of nature and cosmology for thinkers such as Hera-clitus and Democritus, where the configuration of atoms consisted precisely in their patterned modalities of movement. The *rhythm of atoms* would then describe the configurations of matter in motion as *fluid forms* (1971: 286). The tastes of bitterness and sweetness, for example, in Democritus are importantly related to the character of the atomic aggregate being eaten and how it comes into contact with sense organs (O'Keefe, 1997: 119–123). In our terms, the contraction of an atomic pattern would consist in a series of repeated motions (repetition) in a context of some type of flow (difference) according to a particular modality (measure, judgment) and through this accomplishing a temporary configuration (rhythm). As Thanos Zartaloudis argues, Heraclitus offered an ontological vision of difference, repetition, and rhythm in a cosmological framework which saw no strong boundary between *cosmos* and *nomos*. Discussing Heraclitean *nómos* and its relation to nature, Zartaloudis affirms that we must hear in Heraclitean *nómos* 'a dynamic rhythm' precisely insofar as this is what characterises nature, and there is no in-principle distinction between *nómos* and nature (2020: 211; Kahn, 1979: 15). Rhythm has ontological significance in our understanding of patterns and flows from the cosmological to the social, where the distinction between these two is at most a distinction of scale.

This *pre-Platonic* ῥυθμός (*rhuthmós*), then, designates *contingent* material, kinetic, and atomic configurations, as well as their aesthetically accessible *impermanent* and *singular* compound forms in the context of ontological flux and movement (Sauvanet, 1999: 5). So, what did Plato's intervention in the use of ῥυθμός consist in? Perhaps the key point to initially highlight pertains to how Plato's usage of rhythm relates to the *resolution* or *consolidation* of the configurations of movements into an *ordered sequence*. For Benveniste, Platonic rhythm names those properly ordered sequences, time-bound, proceeding through *intervals* determined by μέτρον (*métron*, meter, measure), and as such 'numerically regulated' (1971: 287).

Benveniste cites three primary sites at which we can evidence this Platonic transmutation of ῥυθμός – from the *Philebus* (Plato, 1993), the *Symposium* (Plato, 2008), and the *Laws*. We will consider the *Philebus* (16c2–3) first in the context of a reflection on the proper method of dialectic, through which is manifested the principles of art (*technê*) (Carone, 2011: 81). The initial examples Socrates gives here are *sonic* (speech and music), emphasising the dialectical approach as one which can grasp sonorous highs and lows, as well as their arrangements into intervals proportioned and limited by number, calling these *harmonies*. Socrates analogises this (*Phil.* 17d) to the *motions* or movements of the body which are regulated by number and must be called *rhythms* and *measures* (or meters) (1971: 286). Second, in the *Symposium* (187), rhythm is conceptualised in parallel to harmony in the context of music. Harmony is described as a *consonance* or *agreement* emerging from a prior difference between the grave and the acute, where *harmonisation* is the *resolution* of this difference. In the same way, rhythm is described as the resolution of the fast and the slow. Harmony and rhythm are thus positioned as forms of musical, motional, kinetic, and sonic resolution producing sonic and motional agreement or consonance (1971: 287; also see Green, 2015). Finally, Benveniste (1971: 287) cites the *Laws* (664e–665a) in which rhythm is named as that which exhibits control or order in movement and harmony as that which exhibits control or order of voice, the combination of these taken together being *choral dance* or *choristry*. Rhythm and harmony are gifts from the gods in the attainment of motional and sonic order. Gathering these threads together, Benveniste highlights the key components of Platonic rhythm as the proper (i.e., bound by number and measure) intervallic oscillation between the slow and the fast. We see a mathematisation of rhythm's *binding* function, where the principle of binding relates to synchrony and symmetry, usually closely related to harmony as an *ordered sequence of movements*. Rhythm pertains to 'everything which presupposes continuous activity broken by meter into alternating intervals' (1971: 287). Pascal Michon has named this Platonic transmutation and metricisation of ῥυθμός as one which enabled its mathematical universalisation (2018: 28–33).

It will also be useful to turn to the one use of ῥυθμός in the *Timaeus* (47d–e) not explicitly discussed by Benveniste. The titular character of the dialogue is in this context discussing the faculties of sight and hearing with respect to their function and purpose. Sight's divine function, exhibited through its rational usage, is in the observation of the skies, stars, and sun. Through vision, we see the coming-to-be and passing away of night and day, the revolving years, and so forth, enabling knowledge of number and the study of time (*Tim.* 47a). Visibility (the study of the motions of the sky) is an access point through which to perceive and know the invisible (the study of number). The *telos* of vision is precisely that we use it to know the revolutions or circuits (periods) in the heavens, and to as much an extent as possible imitate these revolutions in our own soul, aligning ourselves to the divine element in us and to that which connects us to such heavenly motions (*Tim.* 47b–c). In just the same way, the *telos* of sound is to enable us to observe, know, and produce sonic and motional imitations in ourselves as a copy of these divine motions. Harmony and rhythm are described as given by the Muses not for irrational pleasure, but as an 'ally against the inward discord that has come into the revolution of the soul, to bring it into order and consonance with itself' (*Tim.* 47d; Cornford, 1997: 158). Sonological and motional order (harmony and rhythm) has a kinetic process analogous to (though remaining an *imitation* of) cosmological order.

Pre-empting elements of our later discussion in this chapter, it is on these grounds and through this function of divine motional imitation that Plato will introduce rhythm and harmony as pedagogical principles in the context of what we will describe as the rhythmic governance of the metronomic *polis* imagined in the *Laws*, where no citizen must be allowed to 'abandon this discipline of number' (*Laws*. 747a). There is a devotion to number, symmetry, and synchrony, and it is fair to call Plato's imagined city-state as *metronomic*. The purpose of law and the task of the lawgiver is to bring about measured kinetic order at the level of the citizen's everyday life. At the beginning of Book 2 of the *Laws* (653a–654b), education is defined as a training in habits (repetitions) in such a way that one's habitual motions are *pre-reflectively* attuned with reason, and this consonance will be further realised should education in reason itself lead to a recognition of the harmony between the motions of the body and the motions of the soul. This begins with affective training for the management of pleasures and pains, and religious festivals are framed as such a training ground in this pedagogy of the body-soul. The Muses, Apollo, and Dionysus are fellow-celebrants and participators in this pedagogy. We will return to this later. But we can note for now that the untrained soul is motionally and sonically discordant, producing disordered sounds and gestures. Humans, the Athenian claims (paralleling the previous claim made in the *Timaeus*), have been given the perception of order and disorder (that is, how to perceive rhythm and harmony). Religious festivals (themselves cyclic practices) enable pleasure to be extracted from an appropriate source (rhythm and harmony) in the education of the soul. The cyclical nature of the festival can also be considered as itself a social mode of motional imitation to the divine, given that cyclicity entails the regulated ordered repetitions of these practices consonant with the cycles of the heavenly bodies.

The nomological significance of the festival is due to the fact that the education of the soul is the central task of the lawgiver. This training ground of the soul is vital in the preparation for citizenship, as producing sonic and motional movements attuned to the divine *is* the production of excellence of soul and body (*Laws*. 665b). Law is concerned with the distribution of kinetic order, and rhythm will become a principle of kinetic regulation for the Athenian's imagined lawgiver given its educational importance and divine significance.

With some contextualisation now given of the etymological debates and context of Plato's usage of rhythm, we will now turn in more detail to cosmological and nomological order, beginning with the former.

§10 Rhythmanalytical Notes on Plato's *Timaeus*

Plato's *Timaeus*, generally considered among the "late" dialogues, is primarily a monologue delivered by the titular (and most likely fictional) character from Locri, southern Italy, whose positions have been strongly compared to the natural philosophy of Philolaus of Croton, a prominent Pythagorean (Riedweg, 2005: 117). Both the immensity of the influence as well as the complexity of content of this dialogue necessitate that this section can only briefly highlight some of the key components important for our purposes. We will devote ourselves prominently to outlining the different *scales* of order and motion envisaged in this cosmological picture.

The *Timaeus* mixes cosmogenetic myth and cosmological treatise, giving an account (*logos*, λόγος) of the *cosmos* (*kosmos*, κόσμος) (the visible, ordered, and beautiful whole or universe), blending creation myth with philosophy. The dialogue "concludes" at the creation of humans. The cosmos is imagined as *organic*, that is, as 'a living creature with soul and reason' (*Tim.* 30b–c). The purposes of such a cosmological treatise are ontological, epistemological, but importantly normative. This cosmological-normative nexus is apparent in two key senses.

First, the principal agential and creative force in the creation myth is the "Demiurge", the craftsman of the cosmos imparting Reason upon cosmic motions: the cosmos is a continuously moving work of art with elements of designed purpose. The Greek term for the craftsman here used (δημιουργός) referred largely and broadly to skilled practice, for example, sculpting, medicine, or cookery, but it also had a political sense. In the *Republic* (Plato, 2000) (507c), the term is used in both senses, referring to the maker of our senses (sight, hearing) and of the ratios of the motions of the stars (530a–c), knowledge of which is necessary to properly function as lawgivers. The philosopher-ruler in the *Republic* is referred to as a *demiurge* of justice, moderation, and virtue who, as Gabriela Roxana Carone notes, 'orders the state, the citizens, and himself according to goodness' (2011: 8; 500d).

The demiurgic function crucially pertains to the proper *ordering* of motion: ordering celestial or sublunary motions towards order from discordance or ordering kinetic and sonic motion in the *polis*. As Kalkavage notes in his translation (2006: 15), in the *Timaeus* (30a), this "pre-cosmic" discordance is an out-of-tuneness or lack of musicality (*plêmmêlôs*, πλημ-μελής), a term Plato also uses in the *Laws* to denote various *discordances* of the individual (when the soul does not follow knowledge) and city (when the population does not follow rulers and laws). The greatest *concord*, as adherence to cosmological harmony, is described as wisdom (Zartaloudis, 2020: 368; *Tim*. 47b–e; *Laws*. 689b-d).

The *telos* of demiurgic craftsmanship is to order motions given the contingencies which limit it. The Demiurge is not omnipotent. The cosmos is not fully ruled by the Reason the Demiurge institutes, and a significant feature of the *Timaeus* is the manner in which the cosmic realm (of Becoming) consists of a mixture of Reason (Soul) and Necessity (chance), the most obvious example of which is the mix of soul and body in the human (*Tim*. 47e–48b). Associating Necessity with "chance" may sound awkward to our ears, but this distinction pertains on the one hand to that which occurs with *telos* (e.g., craftsmanship) and on the other to that which occurs without *telos*. Necessity and chance name the same thing in this context, as Cornford highlights with reference to Plato and Aristotle (Cornford, 1997: 165–167). That which occurs without designed *telos* is that which happens of Necessity or chance, to be contrasted with the *order* the Demiurge seeks to institute through Reason.

This brings us to the second sense of the cosmological-normative nexus. The Demiurge's craftsmanship is effectuated with reference to a *model* found in the realm of Being (that uncaused realm which is permanent, eternal, and unchanging, and of which knowledge can be attained through reason, dialectic, and mathematics). The cosmos is a realm of Becoming and is impermanent, temporal, always changing, and of which only sense-perception and (constitutively unreliable) judgments and beliefs are possible. For example, it is only in the realm of Becoming that *time* is produced and its *measurement* is possible (Cornford, 1997: 26). Time is defined famously in the *Timaeus* as produced by the ordered movements of the planets and as a 'moving likeness of eternity . . . moving according to number' (*Tim*. 37D; Carone, 2011: 34). It is the Demiurge who instituted this accordance or concordance with number (i.e., as a copy made with Being as its normative model). Time itself, as a moving and ordered sequence bound to number, is as such contingent upon the Demiurge's cosmic craftsmanship.

While the notion of rhythm is at times remote in the *Timaeus*, it must not be forgotten that rhythm is itself an ordered sequence of movements. Harmony plays a more important role in the *Timaeus*, but we have already evidenced the extent to which Plato would often couple these terms together. A question remains: of what do these various motional imitations consist, and what is the character of their processes? Generally speaking, in the *Timaeus*, there are seven types of motion, which can be first divided into two kinds. The first is the *circular*, expressive of that movement which is most ordered, rational, regular, and uniform; the second is the *rectilinear*, divisible into six (up, down, forward, backward, left, right), expressive of movement which is disordered, irrational, wandering, and irregular (Cohen, 2020: 94–95). The circular and rectilinear exist across cosmic scales. Given this, our frame of analysis will discuss motion primarily in terms of their scales, what we describe as three *modes* of motion: the macrocosmic, the microcosmic, and the mesocosmic.

§10.1 Macrocosmic Motions

Macrocosmic motions pertain to the shape and movement of the cosmos taken, first, as a whole and, second, as the revolutions of the celestial bodies.

The "whole" must be approached through how the Demiurge fashions the World-Soul and World-Body. The World-Body is shaped by the Demiurge as a *sphere*, which is then spun and thereby turns around uniformly upon its axis (*Tim.* 33b–34a). This recursive axial rotation is the motion most proper to reason, and the spherical figure is one that enables it to comprehend all other figures within it. This revolving circular motion is attributed to the World-Soul, which extends throughout and envelops the cosmos (*Tim.* 34a–b). Ontologically, the World-Soul is composed of an compound of Existence, Sameness, and Difference, which partakes in both realms of Being and Becoming (Cornford, 1997: 59–66).

This compound, imagined as a long strip, is then divided into portions/lengths according to two geometric progressions – 1, 2, 4, 8 and 1, 3, 9, 27 – which can be imagined in terms of one long strip (or string) in the order 1, 2, 3, 4, 8, 9, 27. Intervals remain after this division, which are filled with further portions of the compound calculated according to the "arithmetic" and "harmonic" means. Further intervals remain (of 3:2, 4:3, and 9:8), and are filled, at the end of which, all of the intermediate compound has been used up, with a leftover interval of 256:243 (the *leimma*, or remnant) in Pythagorean tuning (Plato, 2016: 20). There are too many elements of geometric and musical importance for us to cover here, but this process is the Demiurge's *skilled tuning* of the World-Soul so that it may have the most proper harmonic structure. Harmony here is primarily *structural* and related to geometric *proportion;* there is no mention in the *Timaeus* of audible cosmic music.

Moving, secondly, to the revolutions of the celestial bodies, this harmonically divided strip is split and bent into two circles – the Circle/ Revolution of the Same and the Circle/Revolution of the Different (*Tim.* 36b–c) – forming the paths according to which planetary bodies move. All these bodies partake in circular (rational) motion.

The Circle of the Same (CS) is the entire movement of the cosmic sphere upon which *all* planetary motions are included and which constitutes the closest imitation to the circular motion proper to reason enveloping the cosmos: it is 'always thinking the same things about the same things' (*Tim.* 40a–b). While all seven planets partake in their own expressions of the Circle of the Different (CD), it is the Sun (whose circle presides over Earthly cycles) which is the most exemplary and significant of these (Cornford, 1997: 83). Celestial motions are divine motions, expressive of the Demiurge's measured judgment as to their ordering.

It is ordering of celestial motions, recall, that *constitutes* cosmic time, making astronomy and the study of mathematics possible and upon which secure knowledge (rather than belief) as well as normative action can be thereby grounded. These *macrocosmic motions* are thus the exemplary normative model for the organisation of the *polis*.

§10.2 Microcosmic Motions

Turning to *microcosmic motions*, principally of the four primary bodies (fire, air, water, and earth), recall that the *telos* of demiurgic craftsmanship is to order motions and movements to the best possible extent given extant limitations. There are two central limitations. First, the primary bodies, as the "raw materials", partake in *rectilinear* (that is, irrational) motions. Second, the *Receptacle*, which is the foundational *spatial* condition, functions alongside Being as the foundational imitative model, in the production of a cosmos of Becoming by the Demiurge (*Tim.* 50c–d). The Demiurge does not create the Receptacle, and it is neither in the realm of Being nor Becoming, being the space "in which" Becoming (and rectilinear motion) occurs (or provides a *situation, context,* or *seat* for Becoming); it is not sensible, but is that which *receives* qualitative modifications (Sallis, 1999: 98–100). These qualitative modifications are the objects of sense-perception: what we aesthetically *perceive* as fire is the *imitation* of the form of fire in the realm of Becoming and in space (i.e., as received within the Receptacle) (*Tim.* 51c–d).

In the ordering of microcosmic motions from a prior out-of-tuneness, the Demiurge is described as "shaking" and rocking the Receptacle and its contents, through which the primary bodies are configured in terms of shapes and numbers (*Tim.* 52e–53b). Visibility must be present in the cosmos (provided by *fire*), as must solidity (provided by *earth*); *air* and *water* are set between these two, and all four are organised by the Demiurge in a proportionate ratio. This ratio or geometric proportion *binds* them together in such a way that the body of the universe comes into concordance and unity as *one* cosmos (in a manner not dissimilar from how harmony and rhythm, as we saw previously, are described in the *Symposium* as that which blends and binds differences in pitch and speed in the production of music) (*Tim.* 31b–32d). The faces of primary bodies are different configurations of triangles, which are then arranged in terms of different three-dimensional shapes assigned to the four primary bodies – earth being associated with the cube, fire with the pyramid, air with the octahedron, and water with the icosa-hedron. Fire, water, and air are built out of the same triangle and so can transform into each other, whereas earth is built of its own trian-gle and cannot transform into the others (*Tim.* 53c–54d). The order the Demiurge institutes with respect to microcosmic motions here is such that Becoming can be explained in terms of shape and number in motion. Sense-perception cannot be dissociated from the configu-ration of the shape of a particular object of perception (e.g., a flame) and the motions transmitted to organs and then the soul (Cornford, 1997: 268).

§10.3 Mesocosmic Motions

The final mode is *mesocosmic motions*, specifically those of the human organism. The human body is fashioned first through the sphere of the head (imitating the cosmic sphere) through which the human can partake in the circular motion of reason and orderliness (*Tim.* 44d–e). There is a *motional* epistemology implied here, where knowledge and belief are significantly related to the epistemic motions of the soul (*Tim.* 37b; Cornford, 1997: 95–97; Carone, 2011: 59). The body (which is a rectilinear vehicle for the head) contains the two mortal parts of the soul: the "spirited" part in the heart, the seat of emotional/affective life (*Rep.* 409c–412a) and the "appetitive" part in the stomach, the seat of desires and drives.

The relative proximity to the head matches the extent to which these parts of the soul can be attuned by or governed through reason. However, it is of note here that the intestines are identified as a *receptacle* which slows the speed of digestion in such a way as to make the time required to practice philosophy possible (*Tim.* 69e–73a). The life of the body is maintained by the circular thrust of respiration involving the rhythmic oscillating interactions of primary bodies (fire and air) and the moving of blood (produced by fire "cutting" food in the digestive process). Ultimately, natural death occurs through the decay of the integrity of the triangles (and the *bond* holding them together) of the primary bodies constituting the organism, which in death let go of the bond to the soul (*Tim.* 78d–79e; 80d–81e). In the absence of atomic *binding*, the life-rhythms of the human organism fade.

It is important to note that we cannot reduce the microcosmic and mesocosmic to the macrocosmic. There is neither complete structural analogy nor motional isomorphism between them. Both Reason and Necessity are present at all scales, having distinctive relative effects. Each scale presents the *solution* arrived at by the Demiurge in an attempt to order the movements of the cosmos. Humans need not follow the circles of Reason, however, and the mortal elements of its constitution (as when being overtaken by certain affects or appetites) can produce disorder in their motions (Carone, 2011: 58–62).

§10.4 From Cosmos to Nomos

In moving towards our next section where our focus will pivot to the *Laws*, it is important to highlight the nomological significance of this vision of divine craftsmanship ordering the motions of the cosmos in relation to Necessity. The task of Plato's lawgiver is to produce a context in which humans follow the divine circles of Reason. The form of the narrative of the dialogue concerns the three characters journeying towards a shrine of Zeus, the object of discussion being the laws (institutions, customs, *nomoi*) and the political context (*politeia*). This is attuned to the dialogue's main object in terms of its content: the harmonising of nomological and cosmological order. So attuned, law (*nomos*) becomes that which is distributed (*dianomê*) by reason (*nous*), law naming those 'provisions made by reason' (*Laws.* 713e–714a). Laws are also measured and calculated, identified as 'political measures' analogous to musical measures (*nomoi* referring to both law and musical measure) (*Laws*. 722d–e). Proper measurement is vital to ensure the city is properly *bound* and maintains temporal integrity and continuity over time (*Laws*. 793b–d), which requires the application of reason (*nous*) and imitation of cosmic ordering (Carone, 2011: 161–162). The *Laws* is thus founded upon a rejection of the image of a cosmos operating only of Necessity. Reason and purposive (though not omnipotent) design, observable in the visible and tangible cosmos instituted by the Demiurge, provide us with a model to imitate when crafting our juridico-political systems: *nomogenesis* is conceived as a moving likeness of *cosmogenesis*. The lawgiver's task is to seek to fashion order in the sphere of human relations in the context of contingency just as the Demiurge's seeks to institute cosmic order in the context of Necessity.

§11 Rhythmanalytical Notes on Plato's *Laws*

Plato's *Laws* is a dialogue concerned with the justification of law in general to detailed construction of particular laws. Cleinias from Crete is part of a party of lawgivers for *Magnesia*, a new Cretan colony (*Laws*. 702b–d; 848b). Cleinias, Megillus from Sparta, and an unnamed Athenian theoretically act as Magnesia's primary lawgivers. The dialogue's task is therefore that of lawgiving or, more specifically, *good* lawgiving: the point is not simply to create laws but to create the best laws possible. This covers areas which we would now call administrative and constitutional law (e.g., when defining and distributing public offices); company, property, and tax law (e.g., discussions on business activity, inheritance, and property-ownership); as well as family law and the question of the purposes of citizenship and education. Child-rearing takes place in the household, but it is by no means simply a private affair: it is primarily a task of public law and education as training for citizenship. There are also substantial portions of the dialogue devoted to penal legislation, judicial procedure, tort, and damages, as well as legal review. While trying not to be too anachronistic in applying contemporary categories here, it is nonetheless important to note that Plato deals with all of these themes in an integrated framework whereby he seeks to put the broadest elements of the scope of the project (that of the ground of law's authority and that of the purpose of legal institutions and practices) in rational harmony and synchrony with the narrowest.

The beginning of the dialogue provides a theological framing of the ground and authority of legal institutions. The opening question concerns to whom credit ought to be given for the legal arrangements of the cities represented in the discussion: humans or the gods? The Spartan and the Cretan agree that such responsibility should be accorded to the relevant gods (Zeus for Crete, Apollo for Sparta). Likely situated in the mid-4th century BC, the three characters are hiking from Knossos to the cave of Zeus beginning around dawn and at some point in the year near the summer solstice. The cave of Zeus is, as described by Mark Munn (2013: 32), 'the place of origin of the most ancient laws known to the Greeks, the laws that Minos, first king of Knossos, received from Zeus, his father'. Eric Salem (2013: 49) frames this hike as an ascension from 'effect to cause, from convention to nature'. In both word and deed, this is to say, the three characters are searching for the source and purpose of lawgiving.

Our exploration of the *Laws* in this section will take a similar approach to our discussion of *Timaeus*. Here, we will differentiate again between three scales of motion: the cosmological, the institutional (or social), as well as that of the citizen in everyday life. In the *Laws*, these three scales are those which the lawgiver must consider, devising principles thereon, and then distributing these principles across these three scales for their proper synchronisation and alignment.

§11.1 Scale 1: The Cosmological

Early in the *Laws*, the unnamed Athenian (who, it should be noted, is never named as Socrates) opens the discussion into the *purpose* of laws (*nomoi*), institutions and customs (*nomina*), and political arrangements (*politeia*). Both the Cretan and the Spartan attest to a view that these institutions have been designed with an eye to war, understanding peacetime in a proto-Hobbesian sense of an undeclared war of all against all (*Laws*. 626a), before the Athenian counters that such design ought to be made with an eye to what is *best* or to the good. What is best cannot be simply the waging of war, as 'war is not waged for its own sake but for the sake of the fruits of victory' (Strauss, 1977: 6). There are two types of goods mentioned: human (health, good looks, strength, and wealth) and divine (wisdom, self-control, justice, and courage). Divine goods are part of the natural order, ranking them higher on the hierarchy of goodness. The good lawgiver must aim to become an executor of the natural rule of law (Strauss, 1977: 9) as the proper purpose of lawmaking will be to create the context for human and divine goods such that these divine goods are, as much as possible, attainable. Divine goods have this higher status insofar as they are *prior to* (logically and temporally) or are a *condition of* human goods.

This account of divine goods and their status rests on a description of the *motion* of primary bodies in the cosmos, particularly in Book 10, wherein the unnamed Athenian becomes concerned with impiety and the refutation of atheism. The ensuing discussion providing this description, it is important to underline, is itself codified as part of the written legal code in the form of a prelude (discussed further in §11.3). This prelude is a *rationale* or *ratio* for the black letter law on impiety and atheism.

A key source of impiety and atheism is identified as a false understanding of the nature of primary (fire, water, air, earth) and planetary bodies. The atheist understands the make-up and motion of such bodies as lifeless and explained by chance (*Laws*. 889a–c). In the atheist's cosmology, *chance* comes before *craftsmanship*, the latter being considered as pertaining to 'playthings which have very little to do with truth' (*Laws*. 889d–e). For the atheist, *lawgiving* is akin to art and divorced from truth. The unnamed Athenian is concerned about the relativistic dangers which flow from such an atheistic cosmology: the gods and the good are both understood as conventional, subject to modification depending on time, place, situation, and so on. From the starting point of an atheistic cosmology, the consequences are a relativistic legal system and, inevitably, social unrest and instability with no stable model which political and legal institutions can imitate (*Laws*. 889e–890a).

For the unnamed Athenian, the atheist logically misidentifies the primary source of motion, which is not bodies or chance, but the soul (as the capacity for self-motion) (*Laws*. 895e–896c). It is the soul whose motions provide 'an inexhaustible flow of existence' and impose order (*Laws*. 966e).

The motion most appropriate to the (good) soul is that of the circle, or otherwise analogised to a sphere turned on a lathe in a spinning rotation with its centre distributing the same motions throughout (unlike the bad soul, which moves in a 'frenzied, disordered way' [*Laws*. 897d]). Pointing to the planetary bodies, the Athenian notes that the soul which is the principle of the sun's motion must be regarded as a god (*Laws*. 899a). The ordered motions visible in the sky are further identified as empirical reasons to refute the atheist's chance-centric cosmology, as well as that through which citizens can observe and thus imitate such order in their own lives. Even when, earlier in the dialogue in Book 7, Cleinias observed that the celestial bodies sometimes appeared to be "wandering" and change course, the Athenian moves to correct him. While planets sometimes appear to us to be moving disorderedly, they are in fact following the same circular path (*Laws*. 822a; *Tim*. 38e–39b; Cornford, 1997: 114).

As Trelawny-Cassity has noted (2014: 339), discussing the image Plato used of circular motion being like a craftsman spinning a sphere on a lathe, 'the dēmiourgoi of the *Laws* are ordinary human beings and not some cosmic creator'. But with the appropriate cosmology, we have an image of divine craftsmanship which lawgivers can imitate in their own demiurgic task.

§11.2 Scale 2: The Institutional

This section will examine the institutional scale in four subsections. First, we will discuss the question of the natural environment and composition of citizenry (§11.2.1). Second, we will address the question of land apportionment (§11.2.2). Third, we will highlight some key juridico-political offices and procedures (§11.2.3). Finally, we will consider the court system and the so-called Nocturnal Council (§11.2.4). Throughout, we will consider how this crafting of institutions is done in such a way that legal institutions and practices both imitate and serve as nodes or connections through which legal/nomological order can synchronise with cosmological order.

§11.2.1 The Materials of Craftsmanship

The local ecology within which the *polis* is situated will have economic and social effects which must be central to the lawgiver's concern. Proximity to the sea will mean more flows in and out of the city, and too many resources will produce too much wealth or too many opportunities (e.g., too much timber for shipbuilding provides too much commercial opportunity [*Laws*. 705a–d]): all the better to be self-sufficient so that the new city-state can self-regulate. Too many inflows and outflows provide more opportunities for citizens to find *bad* models to imitate (other city-states, other models of citizenship), and making 'it difficult to imitate its enemies is no bad thing for a city' (*Laws*. 705c–d). Of course, it is important to note that citizens themselves would be a numerical minority in Magnesia. For example, the city-state is formed primarily upon an exclusionary relationship with respect to slaves. Slavery is a legal institution, and slaves are the condition of the leisure and political life of Magnesia. Permanently excluded from the category of citizenship, slaves are those upon which this imagined city is built and sustained (see Morrow, 1939; Prauscello, 2017: 59–68). While citizens are engaged in the full-time job of citizenship itself, trade and crafts are the concern of strangers (metics) and their slaves (*Laws*. 919d; Prauscello, 2017: 21). Magnesian citizens are not permitted to hold gold or silver (so as to discourage vices related to the pursuit of profit), except to conduct essential everyday business such as paying slaves or immigrants (*Laws*. 741b–742a). 'Slaves and masters', the Athenian counsels, 'can never be friends' (*Laws*. 756e–757a): friendship, which is one of the central aims of the lawgiver and thus of the entire project of lawgiving (*Laws*. 693b–c), is only possible in the context of the (relative) equality between citizens. Slaves and other non-citizens are outside of the public regime of friendship.

Considering further the composition of the citizenry itself – which in the *Statesman* (Plato, 1995) are called the *materials* out of which the statesman constructs a state – the Athenian will even think it impossible to avoid at least some form of proto-eugenicist purge so that the bodies and souls which compose the citizenry are at least amenable to proper education and excellence of soul and body (*Laws*. 735a–736b; *Statesman*. 308d). As has been noted by many, statecraft is conceptualised by Plato as coincident with soulcraft, but proper statecraft-soulcraft cannot be dissociated from having the right materials for demiurgic practice, including having the right kind of body-soul compounds, as well as fitting statecraft within the specific ecology of the territory, all of which are relevant to nomological craftsmanship.

§11.2.2 Sacred Metronomics and the Distribution of Land

In §3, recall that we noted that the distributive dimension of *nomos* pertained to the assigning, apportioning, and distribution of resources and spatial portions, principally food and land. In the *Laws*, land distribution is crucial, having a divine mode of allocation. The participants in the dialogue are discussing the founding of an *apoikia*, that is, a colony or settlement, which was founded with the intention of having its own laws, citizens, and community (Whitley, 2001: 124). In the founding of an *apoikia*, the distribution-sharing of the territory was one of the primary acts, and such a task would often take place under the guidance of the *geōmetrai* (those who measure the land) or the boundary-setters. Founding the *apoikia* was also sacred and often involved enlisting the help of a god (Zartaloudis, 2020: 99–101).

Properly distributing land and establishing boundaries on wealth are essential to ensure the avoidance of disputes. No city can be stable in the presence of excessive proprietary and economic imbalances. In its foundation, the city must abandon the profit motive (*Laws*. 737a–b). While four property classes are mentioned, a floor (the original allocation) and ceiling (four times that) are established for wealth and poverty (*Laws*. 744c–e). The establishment of wealth boundaries is of crucial significance for the lawgiver. Any city without strict and permanent coded boundaries on wealth accumulation and money-making practices is one ripe for disharmony and imbalance, as such inequality equals more litigation, disharmony, and disparity among the citizens. A legal and political system founded on the minimisation of imbalances is one which seeks to minimise litigation and the need for dispute resolution, with dispute resolution itself being more necessary than desirable.

What, to be more specific, is this original property allocation which is permanent and unchangeable? The method of determining this is mathematical: land shall be allocated among 5,040 households (*Laws*. 740a–d). Allocation is not privatisation. Such land is still common and is thus inalienable. The number of apportionments are positioned so as to remain constant through the generations (forbidding, for example, something like property speculation) (Zartaloudis, 2020: 101). After marking off an acropolis for Hestia, Zeus, and Athena, the lawgiver will mark off 10,080 portions of land – and each household will receive two portions of land (one near the centre, one close to the borders), constituting their allocation (*Laws*, 745c–e). The number 5,040 is not an arbitrary one. It enables smooth administration via its highly composite divisibility. It can be divided by 12 twice, and it can be divided by all the cardinal numbers from one to 12 (excepting 11). The 5,040 households are divided into 12 tribes. Each tribe is assigned one of the 12 Olympian deities with respective assigned places for monthly ritual and devotional practices. This divination of the numerical schema of land apportionment, as well as of the 12 tribes, highlights the non-arbitrariness of this numerical schema: the city must in its founding recognise the divinity of the division of the land, for this apportionment is a sacred one and is a matter of cosmorhythmic alignment, 'following the months and revolution of the universe' (*Laws*. 771b).

Festivals, feasts, and sacrifices are juridico-religious events performed by legal officials. There are 12 monthly festivals – with choral performances as well as musical and gymnastic competitions – following the gods to whom tribes have been assigned. There will be no fewer than 365 sacrifices (*Laws*. 828c). The mathematical method of distribution is sacralised through aligning this distribution with religious practices, making metronomic distinctions divine. In Magnesia, all division and distribution, as well as the measurement of units for trade, weight, and so on, will only produce stability when such distribution is founded upon the universality of number. The divine mathematics of metronomic lawgiving is as much about making the lawgivers themselves, but also the citizenship in general, devotees of the 'discipline of number' (*Laws*. 747a).

§11.2.3 Juridico-Political Offices

Turning to legal officials, one of the most important such offices is that of the guardians of the law, of which there will be 37, all of whom ought to be aged between 50 and 70 (with maximum 20-year terms). The 37 guardians have an executive function, ensuring the implementation of laws, and a surveillance function, in which they oversee the land register. If there are disputes regarding improper financial conduct, they also have a judicial function, hearing and deciding cases. Sanctioning is strict for those who step outside property bounds, governing affectively and economically, with guilty convictions bringing humiliation and exclusion from some common resources. Permanent criminal records are also to be kept and made generally available (*Laws*. 754d–755a).

After discussing key military appointments, the Athenian proposes a Council of 360 members. Each of the four property classes can elect 90 members to this Council. Voting is compulsory. Council elections follow a very specific rhythm, and councillors serve one-year terms (*Laws*. 756). The Council itself is divided into 12, with each subdivision taking responsibility for Council duties for one month of the year. The Council members are tasked with supervising the rhythms of the *polis* from sunrise to sunset without break, watching over internal stability and inflows/outflows, with the authority to convene and dissolve regular and emergency assemblies (*Laws*. 756b–758d): their term and function are entirely synchronised with solar rhythms.

The next task involves consideration of other public officials: magistrates and priests (*Laws*. 758d–764c). First, rural commissioners have extensive responsibilities over their two-year terms and merit some attention. For the first year, they command young men in the service of protecting a chosen lot in the countryside, moving to a different lot (eastward/rightward) each month, thereby purposively moving in a circle as the year proceeds. In the second year, this movement is reversed (westward/leftward). Their responsibilities are to secure the territory, taking care of fortifications, as well as roads, irrigation, and other matters, and judging minor disputes (which can, at times, be subject to review). Their manner of life is prescribed as austere, towards the cultivation not just of in-depth knowledge of Magnesia, but also humility. Second, urban commissioners supervise and regulate city public and juridical functions. Third, market commissioners supervise and regulate market processes.

The domains of culture and education are included within this discussion of juridico-political offices because these are crucial domains of soulcraft which, as mentioned previously, is not distinct from statecraft. Two sets of officials are established: the first in charge of physical and intellectual education, and the second of competition in athletics, music, and poetry. These roles are overshadowed by one of the most watchful set of eyes in the *polis:* the Superintendent of Education, who holds membership of a body which oversees the laws and whose office is, 'of the highest offices in the city, by far the most important' (*Laws.* 765e; 915e). The central focus of these officials is educative, social, and physical rituals, and they are particularly concerned with how everyday life is lived (temporally) and experienced (aesthetically), laying out *how* citizens express themselves: the melody, rhythm, and tempo of not just song and dance but of the habits of everyday life (gesture, speech, behaviour).

Discussing education and culture generally, the Athenian emphasises that music (including dance, poetry, and song) is a domain central to the lawgiver's task of crafting excellent body-soul compounds. Kinetic gestures and sonic cadences can be rhythmical or harmonious, and excellent soul-body compounds will exhibit – or indeed are difficult to distinguish from – such rhythm and harmony. Those of excellent soul and body have the right gestures and the right modes of speech, and they imitate the divine in all aspects of their soul-body compound. As such, good modes of gesture and speech attach to excellence of soul and body (*Laws.* 655a–b). The Athenian here praises the freezing of aesthetic experimentation he ascribes to Egyptian artistic practices, where no innovation was permitted, highlighting that the proper lawgiver will be acutely concerned with forming an institution which properly guides citizens as to the appropriate modes of expression (e.g., linguistic, bodily, musical) and pleasures with permanently settled criteria of judgment. As Michon (2018: 60, our addition) describes it, the '"eurhythmization" of society should then penetrate very deeply in the souls [of citizens] by controlling the various kinds of performance of' speech (with emphasis on poetry), but also gesture and movement.

The officials in charge of physical and intellectual education, but especially the Superintendent of Education, therefore, play a most crucial juridical role in the imagined Magnesia, as *conductors* and *choreographers* of citizenship. They delimit and regulate proper practices and expression. The lawgiver, combining statecraft with soulcraft, seeks to institute the rule of law in the souls of the citizens (*Laws*. 960e–d).

§11.2.4 Courts and the Nocturnal Council

In discussing the court system, the Athenian outlines a distinction between private and public law: one will access the former in disputes between citizens and the latter if one accuses a citizen of harming the community (*Laws*. 766d–767c). Stress is placed upon a principle common in considerations of the rule of law: namely, that of *access to the courts*: 'anyone who is excluded from the right to be a part of the judicial process is not going to regard himself as part of the city at all' (*Laws*. 768b).

The imagined system of courts, including plaintiff rights, procedures, appeals, and judicial appointments, are all considered (*Laws*. 956b–e). In cases of public law, all citizens are taken as having suffered a wrong, and the public thus have access to participate in the judicial process. But if agreement cannot be reached, then a decision will be made by three senior officials which the prosecutor and defendant agree upon (Strauss, 1977: 91). In Book 12, the Athenian legislates on an entire code of civil and criminal procedure, as well as on damages and their recovery. Legal codes, procedures, but also judges themselves are that which keep the 'city on the straight and narrow': guiding motionally discordant bodies and souls towards appropriate sonic and kinetic motions and 'releasing' bad souls from their own lack of justice (bad opinions, no self-control, cowardice) (*Laws*. 957d–e).

The final aspect of the institutional scale we will highlight here is the final one mentioned in the *Laws*, which is unfortunately only discussed in relatively scant detail: the *Nocturnal Council*, described as a 'night-time council of magistrates' (*Laws*. 968a–b) who meet in the night-time, likely three "hours" before sunrise (Wallace, 1989). Composed of the most excellent citizens in the city (including the current and previous Superintendents of Education, elders from the law guardians, prize-winning priests, potentially certain envoys, and certain invited younger citizens being considered as potential future members), the Nocturnal Council's central task is to discuss and suggest potential improvements to the law, exploring possibilities for enriching the study and practice of lawgiving and receiving reports from the previously mentioned envoys on fact-finding missions to contribute to this (*Laws*. 951c-952b; 947a). The Nocturnal Council members are described as an *anchor* for Magnesia, ensuring it repeats the proper motions daily and yearly, and that the law keeps the city's *telos* in view, 'keeping its eye fixed on a single target' (*Laws*. 962d). They also certainly have knowledge of cosmology and theology. They are imagined as serving a partly correctional purpose. One of the three city prisons is placed near their meeting place, named the "prudentiary". If a judge sentences citizens with impiety for reasons of folly (rather than bad disposition or character), they can be sent to the prudentiary, during which time the Nocturnal Council members are their reformers: the precise intersection with statecraft and soulcraft, where the correction of souls is at the same time the correction of the city's *telos* (*Laws*. 907e–909a). The Nocturnal Council (discussed further in §12) is that conduit through which its members can attain the immortality and immutability which Plato dreams of for Magnesia (*Laws*. 960d).

§11.3 Scale 3: The Citizen

Education – as the most crucial component of statecraft-soulcraft – is training for citizenship. It is directed, from childhood, towards goodness and justice such that the soul-body is animated by 'a desire and a passion to become a complete citizen' (*Laws*. 643e). As Lucia Prauscello notes, citizenship is a full-time job: 'Magnesian citizens will then practice only one *technē* : the *technē* of virtue that quite literally coincides with the "craft of citizenship"' (2017: 21–22; quoting Morrow, 1960: 322). A positive program of education is thus central to public law, and while modes of rational persuasion are important, this program nonetheless puts front and centre *desire* as a central object of law's soulcraft. This *affective* governance concerns, to recall §9, training the citizen's management of and relationship to pleasures and pains which is 'propaedeutic to and compatible with rational understanding' (Prauscello, 2017: 86). Our focus will be on the ways in which this training can be understood as forwarding a *musical form of citizenship*. Citizenship is musical in the *Laws* in four senses: temporal, aesthetic, motional, and participatory. The life of the citizen can be understood as a *temporal* movement with the *aesthetic* telos of order, achieved through *motion*al regulation (particularly *kinetic, sonic,* and *rational*) and *participation* in ordered movements (e.g., obeying the law and ritual performances).

However, for the life of the citizen to be properly ordered, a key problem the lawgiver faces is that of *persuasion*. As we know from the *Timaeus* (48A), the cosmos contains a mixture of Reason and Necessity, and an ordered cosmos evidences Necessity having been *persuaded* by Reason towards the telos of order. The lawgiver faces an analogous problem to the Demiurge: how, in the context of Necessity, to successfully mix in Reason for attainment of order in the city and the 'friendly co-operation of its varied parts' (Morrow, 1950: 162). In lawgiving, persuasion is *not* simply epistemological. We will explore it here first, through kinetic and sonic regulation (e.g., music and gymnastics) and second, on rational persuasion found in the *preludes* of the proposed Magnesian constitution and in developing our reading of musical citizenship. It must be emphasised that musicality is not simply a metaphor or analogue for ordered motion. Music in the ancient Greek sense is far from its sense in contemporary hyper-industrial capitalism. The focus of the latter often restricts music to the domain of producing musical objects and their attentional consumption. The focus of the former, however, pertains to any art over which the Muses presided (that is, poetry, dance, music), but it generally cannot be strongly dissociated from the everyday. Giovanni Comotti, addressing the musicality of Greek culture itself, notes that the 'simultaneous presence of music, dance, and word in almost all forms of communication suggests also the existence of a widespread musical culture among the Greek peoples from the remotest times' (1977: 5; also see Babich, 2005; Heaney, 2019). Indeed, as Zartaloudis notes (2020: 369), '"Being", one could say, for the early Greeks, is not only "said in many ways", but is rhythmopoietic. The kosmos, in this sense, has an acoustic-melic signature which was heard in everyday speech, or mousike'. In this sense, we can imagine everyday life, but certainly festivals, rites, and rituals, as *participatory* and *musical*. Although not discussing ancient Greece, Turino defines what he terms participatory performance and music quite usefully for our purposes: participatory music is music as social interaction with priority on the *process of performance*, rather than the creation of a musical object of consumption. It focuses on the 'sonic and kinesic interaction among participants' in which 'stylized sound and motion are conceptualized . . . as heightened social interaction', facilitating the forging and strengthening of affective bonds (Turino, 2008: 28).

Rituals and festivals are legally programmed into everyday life in Magnesia such that everyday life itself, choreographed by these institutional calendars, can as much as possible become an imitation of and ode to the cosmos. What, then, will be the positive program of education in order for Magnesian citizens to attain such daily devotion?

Beginning with care in both infancy and early childhood, Rachana Kamtekar (2010: 143) highlights the idea that the soul of the child who needs to be guided is characterised by unruly motion, and as such, the pedagogical project is 'in terms of channeling these disorderly movements to get them back on course'. An infant's fearful motions are calmed through rocking, and the act of rocking is a training for courage which enables the child to learn the movement from fear to calm (the overcoming of fear) through rhythmic and motional regulation. This process is also a conduit to the gods and is of divine significance. Order is experienced and developed through the sense of rhythm and harmony. The Athenian notes:

> What the story says is that pretty well any young creature is incapable of being quiet, either physically or vocally; it has to be trying to move and make sounds all the time, now jumping and skipping (dancing for pleasure, for example, or playing games), now uttering all kinds of sounds. Other creatures, we are told, have no perception of order or disorder – what we call rhythm and harmony – in these motions. But in our case, the gods we said were given to us to be our companions in the dance – they are also the ones who have given us the ability to take pleasure in the perception of rhythm and harmony. This is their way of moving us and acting as our chorus-leader, joining us with one another through song and dance.
>
> (*Laws*. 653d–654a)

In the *Timaeus* (88A–89C), we are told that excellence of soul and body is achieved through a proportionate balance between exercising soul and body. Both must be subject to a regime where each 'will imitate what we have called the foster-mother and nurse of the universe'. One must perpetually keep the body in motion, constantly shake the body, and through this bring the body 'into orderly arrangement . . . such as we described in speaking of the universe'. One will recall how, in the ordering of microcosmic motions from that "initial" state of out-of-tuneness, the Demiurge is described as "shaking" and rocking the Receptacle and its contents, through which the primary bodies are configured in terms of shapes and numbers. The ultimate success (or lack thereof) of the public education program of soulcraft is the decisive factor in the city attaining immortality through its daily, monthly, and annual repetitions and cycles: in how the souls and bodies are continuously being shaken and put into order from (and indeed before) infancy. As Strauss notes, for example, 'the permanence of the laws depends on the permanence, the unchangeability, of children's games and playthings; for only in this way can they learn from the very beginning to esteem what is old and to scorn what is new' (1977: 103). Magnesia at times waivers between the image of a city as potentially permanent as the celestial bodies themselves, but there is also the persistent concern to always channel disorder into order. In Book 7's discussion of games, the Athenian describes with fear the revolutionary child:

> Those children who are revolutionaries when it comes to games are inevitably going to grow up into different men from their predecessors; having grown up to be "other" they will try and find themselves another kind of life; and having tried to find that, they set their hearts on different laws and different ways of behaving.
>
> (*Laws.* 978c)

Such disorder and play are, of course, unacceptable in Magnesia. While in infancy and early childhood, motional order is distributed through rocking, the juridical goal of this kinetic pedagogy of citizenship – called by André Laks a 'kinetics of virtue' (1988: 220; Prauscello, 2017: 146) – is that each citizen is capable of self-motion. Again, in the *Timaeus* (89A), we are told that the best motion is that which is 'produced in oneself by oneself, since it is most akin to the movement of thought and of the universe'.

Physical training in the developing citizen involves dancing and wrestling, the former being concerned with the form of imitation (representation) and the latter with the functional aspects of imitation (fitness, agility, strength, balance). Suitable functional training will allow proper 'contraction and extension of the limbs and body parts themselves, and the transmission of rhythmical movement from one part to another' (*Laws.* 795e). Suitable representative training, for example, in choral performances, as Prauscello highlights, will 'only involve the imitation of states of character and actions that are proper of the good citizen' (2017: 139). This is why comedies must only be performed by slaves and foreigners (*Laws.* 816e; or see Prauscello, 2017: 62–64), so citizens do not participate in motional imitation of what is ridiculous or ludicrous.

Citizens must study the ridiculous, so they know what to avoid, but they cannot imitate it. The Athenian in this way offers a whole typology of gestural and rhythmic forms appropriate to bodily movement decisive in the formation of a properly ordered soul and body. The organisation of choral performances further highlights the rhythms and kinetics of Magnesia's musicalised form of citizenship. These are split into three: with the first being the Muses' chorus comprising children, the second being those up to age 30 who invoke Apollo Paean as their healer, and the third being men between 30 and 60 whose patron is Dionysus (*Laws*. 2664c–665b). (Those older than this are thought to now be storytellers, given the fact that their vocal cords and bodies are strained from a lifetime of sonic and kinetic praise to the gods.)

Choral performances are collective devotion and prayer which seek to *enchant* and *persuade* all in the city. Plato also suggested that the laws themselves must be poeticised, set to music, and themselves performed and even danced. Gerard Naddaf (2000: 346) even 'strongly suggests that the entire code of laws is to be set to music, that is, adapted to rhythm and harmony and sung in chorus with the accompaniment of the lyre either collectively or individually'. The Athenian describes these continuous enchantments as the 'city singing to itself' (*Laws*. 665c), and they are participated in and performed by citizens as both imitation of and ode to cosmic order. Dance is a form of *corporeal prayer* (Séchan, 1930: 240, quoted in Naddaf, 2000: 346). Strauss notes that education 'consists then in habituating the child to feel joy and pain in agreement with the law and with those who have been persuaded by the law, or with the old men' (1977: 27). The capacity for kinetic self-motion (which pedagogy aims at) is not at all a kinetic autonomy: the *nomos* or *measure* the citizens regulate themselves with respect to is that laid down by legal institutions and practices: 'no one shall sing a note, or move a step in the dance, other than as laid down by the publicly approved and sacred music, or the general requirements of choral performance by the young – any more than they would contravene any of the other laws or measures' (*Laws*. 799e–800a).

So much for the first mode of persuasion (kinetic and sonic regulation). We will now turn to rational persuasion. The clearest example of this mode is in the *preludes* or *preambles* which prefigure laws. These perform both legal and educative functions: they attach themselves to the penal code in the form of pedagogical documents intended to instruct the citizenry on the rationale or *ratio* of the legal code. The preludes combined with the laws are persuasive in two senses: (i) the preambles provide *ratio* for the law as well as a model to learn, repeat, and imitate as a form of *rational persuasion*, but (ii) they are ultimately backed by the force of the penal code itself, forming a rule to be obeyed, i.e. as a form of *persuasion through rules and their enforcement*. Preambles are analogised to preludes in music and poetry which, we are told, are taken incredibly seriously (*Laws*. 722c–723b). A word for these preludes (*prooimia*), measures, or *preambles* the Athenian uses is *nomoi*. It is the *prelude* (measure, *nomoi*) which is the force of rational persuasion, and it addresses musical citizens in order to enable their investment in the proper sonics, kinetics, and performance of citizenship. We must not expect too much jurisprudential argumentation in the preludes: they are described as geared towards rational persuasion, but this does not unduly limit their form or content. We see, for example, preludes to the marriage laws and to the laws as a whole in Book 5. Our previous discussion on impiety, atheism, cosmology, and primary bodies refers to an extensive prelude discussed in Book 10 – specifically, a prelude to laws on impiety – which is explicitly concerned with rational persuasion. But other preludes, as Julia Annas (2010: 77) points out, 'explicitly appeal to the force of non-rational myths – for example, that the soul of a murdered person will roam the earth seeking vengeance for the crime'. Preambles allow both rational but also affective bonds to be established through the citizen's move towards motional accord with the city. The preambles form a *telos* for good citizens' full-time project of attuning themselves to virtue. Attuning oneself to the laws will, for the virtuous Magnesian citizen, be a lifetime project of kinetic, sonic, and behavioural ordering in everyday life which will, if distributed amongst all citizens, produce a city-state synchronised with each other and with the gods. The citizens' distribution of these motions in their everyday life beats to the repetition of social practice arranged metronomically and regulated by law so as to make the city's annual movements themselves a collective participatory performance, ode, or prayer to the cosmos. Just as the movements of celestial bodies in the *Timaeus* are described as constituting time itself and the possibility of its measurement, the movement of political and social bodies can be described as constituting social time and at the same time as a collective pious and mimetic ritual to that cosmos. So organised, the city can hope to achieve an imitation of the cosmos's own imitation of Being.

§12 Imitating the Cosmos

The power of rhythm pervades Magnesia, whether it is in the rocking of infants and raising of children, dancing, training for gymnastic

or other competitions, in festivals and sacrifices to your neighbour-
hood's assigned deity and the ordered sequence of festivals repeated
year-by-year; or in ensuring the appropriate attitudes at funerals (*Laws*.
800c–801b) as well as the corporeal prayer and singing and dancing
of the laws themselves. (The Magnesian, it seems, really never stops
singing or dancing.) The nomological significance of rhythm is significantly related to the fact that rhythm is that divine gift which allows
the aesthetic experience of order in movement, which can then be
used as a foundation for the cultivation of the appropriate kinetic and
sonic movements of the body, voice, and soul for the purpose of the
attainment of virtue. Just as the Demiurge crafted the cosmos across
macrocosmic, mesocosmic, and microcosmic scales according to mathematical and harmonic principles such that order was distributed and
the cosmos itself was a moving work of art, the lawgiver must craft
a city-state that is properly *synchronised* with this cosmic order via its
institutions and how it manages everyday life for the citizen. Whereas
in the *Timaeus*, a key first step is fashioning the World-Body of the
cosmos (in the shape of a sphere) enveloped by the World-Soul, in
the *Laws*, a key first step is fashioning the body of Magnesia and in the
allocation and distribution of its spatial elements, explained as being
in imitation of the revolutions of the universe (*Laws*. 771b) such that
each portion a citizen has temporary stewardship of is truly a gift from
the gods (a gift, nonetheless, *distributed* by the lawgivers and institutions of Magnesia). (For a schematic plan of Magnesia, see Golding
[1975: 365].) Respecting the *nomos* becomes coincident with respecting the *cosmos*. Magnesian institutions must be designed in such a way
that they centralise the truths and principles of the cosmic order, but
the *polis* itself must be aligned with this order and everyday life must
be lived in praise of this order. This includes, for example, having the
appropriate beliefs about the cosmos and of the motions of planetary
and primary bodies (which, as we highlighted previously, are cemented
in the law-code). These motions are empirically accessible to all citizens (one need not study philosophy to know and imitate them) and
are normatively salient, as the patterns of motion proper to the soul
observable in the heavens can also be detected in music, poetry, and
ethical practice (*Laws*. 967d–968a). Citizens must observe and believe
the right sort of things about the cosmos and use this as a stable framework for their own life.

It is also the case that the institutions themselves are designed
to *temporally* operate in imitation to the cosmos. Recall that in the

Timaeus, the cosmos is created as a sphere in constant rotation, and it is enveloped by the World-Soul, and *(cosmic) time* is produced and constituted by the movements of celestial bodies therein, which are a moving likeness or motional imitation of *number*. In order to imitate such motions, Magnesia is designed to repeat itself in its own circle of the same, much like the Demiurge instituted in the cosmos. In the *Laws*, part of the task is constitutional codification, but the aim of codification is to 'frame a code not in need of future improvement' (Strauss, 1977: 78). Recall that the cosmic movement closest to reason is the circle which is 'always thinking the same things about the same things' (*Tim.* 40a–b). The details for such perpetual social reproduction are thorough: from ensuring the perpetual upkeep of the milieu (e.g., roads, buildings, irrigation, beautification, sanitation, and fortifications), legal rituals of succession, detailed procedures for the allocation of various forms of authority, as well continual replenishment of the spiritual sphere with the entire education program and calendar of festivals. The Magnesian city plan involves spatial distribution, but also a detailed permanent schedule for everyday life. Repetition truly reigns over difference in such a vision of quotidian rhythms. The life of the citizen in everyday life is one we have been reading musically: the choral and metronomic arrangement of the *polis* itself moves year-by-year (with its political, musical, gymnastic, and religious rituals and rotations) in a repetitive cycle. The unchangeability of the law produces a collective aesthetic experience whereby 'there is no memory, even through hearsay, of things ever being any different from the way they are now' (*Laws*. 798b). This unchangeability and irreversibility are central to the legislation on children's games, to give a further example, and in how children learn rhythm, music, and modes of motional imitation and how they must be locked in place and sacralised through the generations. Much like the Demiurge fashioning the cosmos in the context of Necessity, the lawgiver must create a legal system which spirals in a form of self-sameness (fashioning a circle of the same) and which only deviates as a course-correction in the context of Necessity. (Chance so often, the Athenian notes, appears to make our laws for us [*Laws*. 709a–c].) The Nocturnal Council is the agency of maintaining the moving work of art that the city is, and its goal is the continual replenishment and maintenance of social reproduction, ensuring the city continues repeating the circle of the same. Council members are the generational custodians of the theory and practices of lawgiving, who must practice excellence of soul and body and who must embody the city's wisdom, reason, and memory. Their daily task is to be that part of the city which knows the aim, purpose, and function of lawgiving, and 'without it the city will lack intellect and sense perception and hence will act haphazardly in everything' (Strauss, 1977: 178). The daily cycle is of clear biorhythmic and cosmorhythmic significance: the Nocturnal Council meets each day, always one step ahead as jurisprudential supervisees of the circadian and chronopolitical rhythms of everyday life in Magnesia.

References

Annas, J. 2010. Virtue and Law in Plato. In *Plato's Laws: A Critical Guide*. Ed. C. Bobonich. Cambridge: Cambridge University Press, pp. 71–91.

Aristotle. 2016. *Metaphysics*. Trans. C. D. C. Reeve. Indianapolis, IN: Hackett Publishing Company.

Babich, B. E. 2005. The Science of Words or Philology: Music in *The Birth of Tragedy* and the Alchemy of Love in *The Gay Science*. *Rivista di Estetica*, 45(28): 47–78.

Barletta, V. 2016. Rhythm as Form. *Dibur*, 2: 47–55.

Barletta, V. 2020. *Rhythm: Form and Dispossession*. Chicago, IL: University of Chicago Press.

Benveniste, É. 1971. The Notion of "Rhythm" in Its Linguistic Expression. In *Problems in General Linguistics*. Trans. M. E. Meek. Miami, FL: University of Miami Press, pp. 281–288.

Carone, G. R. 2011. *Plato's Cosmology and Its Ethical Dimensions*. Cambridge: Cambridge University Press.

Cohen, N. 2020. The Ethics of the Circular and the Rectilinear in Plato's *Timaeus*. *Ancient Philosophy*, 40: 93–106.

Comotti, G. 1977. *Music in Greek and Roman Culture*. Trans. R. V. Munson. Baltimore, MD: Johns Hopkins University Press.

Cornford, F. M. 1997. *Plato's Cosmology: The Timaeus of Plato*. Indianapolis, IN: Hackett Publishing Company.

Formarier, M. 2013. Ρυθμός, *rhythmos* et *numerus* chez Cicéron et Quintilien. Perspectives esthétiques et génériques sur le rythme oratoire latin. *Rhetorica*, 31: 133–149.

Gerber, D. E. (Ed.). 1999. *Greek Iambic Poetry: From the Seventh to the Fifth Centuries BC*. Cambridge, MA: Harvard University Press.

Golding, N. H. 1975. Plato as City Planner. *Arethusa*, 8(2): 359–371.

Green, J. 2015. Melody and Rhythm at Plato's Symposium 1872. *Classical Philology*, 110(2): 152–158.

Heaney, C. 2019. Tragic Rhythms: Nietzsche and Agamben on Rhythm and Art. *La Deleuziana*, 10: 61–78.

Jaeger, W. 1965. *Paideia: The Ideals of Greek Culture: Archaic Greece, the Mind of Athens*. Trans. G. Highet. Oxford: Oxford University Press.

Kahn, C. H. 1979. *The Art and Thought of Heraclitus*. Cambridge: Cambridge University Press.

Kamtekar, R. 2010. Psychology and the Inculcation of Virtue in Plato's Laws. In *Plato's Laws: A Critical Guide*. Ed. C. Bobonich. Cambridge: Cambridge University Press, pp. 127–148.

Laks, A. 1988. *Loi et Persuasion. Recherche Sur La Structure de La Pensee Politique Platonicienne*. Paris: Université Paris IV. www.theses.fr/1987PA040443.

Meyer-Baer, K. 1953. Psychologic and Ontologic Ideas in Augustine's de Musica. *The Journal of Aesthetics and Art Criticism*, 11(3): 224–230.

Michon, P. 2018. *Elements of Rhythmology: I. Antiquity*. Paris: Rhuthmos.

Morrow, G. R. 1939. *Plato's Law of Slavery in its Relation to Greek Law*. Urbana, IL: University of Illinois Press.

Morrow, G. R. 1950. Necessity and Persuasion in Plato's *Timaeus*. *The Philosophical Review*, 59(2): 147–163.

Morrow, G. R. 1960. *Plato's Cretan City: A Historical Interpretation of the Laws*. Princeton, NJ: Princeton University Press.

Munn, M. 2013. ἔρως and the *Laws* in Historical Context. In *Plato's Laws: Force and Truth in Politics*. Eds. G. Recco and E. Sanday. Bloomington, IN: Indiana University Press, pp. 31–47.

Naddaf, G. 2000. Literary and Poetic Performance in Plato's *Laws*. *Ancient Philosophy*, 20: 339–350.

O'Keefe, T. 1997. The Ontological Status of Sensible Qualities for Democritus and Epicurus. *Ancient Philosophy*, 17: 119–134.

Plato. 1993. *Philebus*. Trans. D. Frede. Indianapolis, IN and Cambridge: Hackett Publishing Company.

Plato. 1995. *The Statesman*. Eds. J. Annas and R. Waterfield. Trans. R. Waterfield. Cambridge: Cambridge University Press.

Plato. 2000. *The Republic*. Ed. G. R. F. Ferrari. Trans. T. Griffith. Cambridge: Cambridge University Press.

Plato. 2006. *Timaeus*. Ed. and Trans. P. Kalkavage. Indianapolis: Hackett Publishing Company.

Plato. 2008. *The Symposium*. Eds. M. C. Howatson and F. C. C. Sheffield. Trans. M. C. Howatson. Cambridge: Cambridge University Press.

Prauscello, L. 2017. *Performing Citizenship in Plato's Laws*. Cambridge: Cambridge University Press.

Renehan, R. 1963. The Derivation of ῥυθμός. *Classical Philology*, 58(1): 36–38.

Riedweg, C. 2005. *Pythagoras: His Life, Teaching, and Influence*. Trans. S. Rendall with C. Riedweg and A. Schatzmann. Ithaca, NY: Cornell University Press.

Salem, E. 2013. The Long and Winding Road: Impediment to Inquiry in Book 1 of the *Laws*. In *Plato's Laws: Force and Truth in Politics*. Eds. G. Recco and E. Sanday. Bloomington, IN: Indiana University Press, pp. 48–59.

Sallis, J. 1999. *Chorology: On Beginning in Plato's Timaeus*. Indianapolis, IN: Indiana University Press.

Sauvanet, P. 1999. *Le Rythme grec: d'Héraclite à Aristote*. Paris: Presses Universitaires de France.

Séchan, L. 1930. *La Danse grecque antique*. Paris: E. De Boccard.

Strauss, L. 1977. *The Argument and Action of Plato's Laws*. Chicago, IL: The University of Chicago Press.

Trelawny-Cassity, L. M. 2014. On the Foundation of Theology in Plato's *Laws*. *Époche: A Journal for the History of Philosophy*, 18(2): 325–349.

Turino, T. 2008. *Music as Social Life: The Politics of Participation*. Chicago: University of Chicago Press.

Wallace, R. W. 1989. ΟΡΘΡΟΣ. *Transactions of the American Philological Association*, 119: 201–207.

Whitley, J. 2001. *The Archaeology of Ancient Greece*. Cambridge: Cambridge University Press.

Zartaloudis, T. 2020. *The Birth of Nomos*. Edinburgh: Edinburgh University Press.

3

The Law of Time and the Temporalities of Lawmaking

§13 Rhythm as Object and Principle (Again)

In Chapter 1, we distinguished between rhythm as object (§4) and as principle (§5). The former takes particular processes and analyses their rhythmic properties. The latter, more general and speculative, makes rhythm into a principle of analysis, and we have centralised how this includes thinking across interacting processual scales (e.g., cosmological, biological, and political). Without seeking to reify this distinction between rhythm as object and rhythm as principle, we will nonetheless deploy it in the service of two distinct discussions in this final chapter. First, in order to explore the potential purchase of rhythmanalysis to law and to legal objects of analysis (§14), we will discuss the phenomenon of *time-standardisation*. We noted in §3 that beginning with rhythm as a principle invites us to begin with the abstract (concepts and categories of analysis and judgment), and it invites cautious speculation in that domain. In §14, we will consider time–standardisation as a technical, legal, and political process, across cosmological and atomic scales, of foundational significance in the structuring of the everyday life of civil time. For the rhythmanalyst, time-standardisation must be put into relation with the everyday, which is why this section will conclude with some reflections on the issue of *working time* in this context. Second, in order to explore the potential that law has in enriching our thinking about rhythm (§15), we will consider the temporalities of lawmaking, discussing the distinction between the courts and the legislature in this area. This section will conceptualise the interactions between these distinct institutional temporalities as in service of the *contraction of juridico-political continuity*. These distinct modalities of law (while ostensibly in tension in various ways) operate at distinct normative *speeds* and with distinct temporal textures, but nonetheless interact

DOI: 10.4324/9781003350231-4

to produce the juridico-political field of stabilised expectation frameworks within which everyday life operates.

§14 Time-Standardisation and the Juridico-Politics of Synchronisation

How ought we conceptualise *time* when thinking about law has been the object of much important work (e.g., Goodrich, 2016; Benyon-Jones and Grabham, 2019; Chowdhury, 2020; McNeilly and Warwick, 2022). Postema (2015: 885), for example, says *time* is 'not only among the conditions of the existence of law', but also 'is of its essence'. Similarly, Mawani (2015: 255) highlights that time is usually considered as simply something law exists "in" or potentially as something that "affects" law. Such framings position law and time as *externally* related. Contra this, Mawani affirms that time is 'ontological, requisite, or constitutive feature of law'. We hope that our approach can be situated in consonance with such work. But why, it can justifiably be asked, add in the seemingly *additional* notion of *rhythm*? Two general points can be made here.

First, law's production of civil time acts as a binding force of temporal synchronisation in the milieu (a synchronisation itself performed in relation to some further element – e.g., the atom and the Sun), and such a production transforms the aesthetics and rhythms of everyday life. Law *distributes* civil time and orders quotidian sonics and kinetics, and in so regulating the conduct of citizens, law is indissociable from the *choreography* of social activity. Second, law provides the background temporal *co-ordination* for social practice: the framework for stable expectation frameworks, legal obligations, accounting for damages, accountability, and so forth. Law rhythmises expectation frameworks by sequencing them and putting them in order, as well as intervening when these expectation frameworks are disturbed, via dispute resolution mechanisms. Rhythm provides an angle through which to explore such synchronisation, distribution, choreography, and synchronisation in the aesthetics and cycles of everyday life.

It is important as a preliminary in this chapter for us to centralise the manner in which civil time forms a key component of the temporal texture of everyday life. Consider Philippopoulos-Mihalopoulos's depiction of what he terms the *lawscape* as coterminous with *spatiality*, arguing that law stretches itself across and *as* social and civil space:

> Law spreads on pavements, covers the walls of buildings, opens and closes windows, lets you dress in a certain way (and not any

other), eat in a certain way, smell, touch or listen to certain things, touch other people in a certain way (and not any other), sleep in a certain space, move in a certain way, stay still in a certain way. In the lawscape, every surface, smell, colour, taste is regulated by some form of law, be this intellectual property, planning law, environmental law, health and safety regulations, and so on. . . . A series of regulations, contractual arrangements, statutes and cases visit you in your bathroom.

(Philippopoulos-Mihalopoulos, 2015: 38–39).

The lawscape is an angle of approach upon law's affective and aesthetic spatiality, but it is also and no less the case that law stretches itself across and *as* social and civil time. The aesthetics of civil time are legally textured; demands upon our time can be specified and are enforceable. Law follows us across and as civil space and time. Consider, for example, title registration systems in land law in English and Welsh law. Sarah Keenan (2019: 146; quoting Kevin J. Gray and Susan Francis Gray [2009: 58]) notes that individual landowners 'do not directly own land, but instead own an "estate" or "slice of time" in land, which is ultimately owned by the Crown'. The estate is as much spatial as temporal. Title registration systems, such as those introduced in the *Land Registration Act 1925* or more comprehensively and recently in the *Land Registration Act 2002*, legislatively smooth the process of conveyancing and open the territory more to the rhythms of the market. The title registration system in this way produced legal space (estates in land) temporally adjusted in the service of accumulative and speculative rhythms. This system also created new modes of temporal co-ordination: in contrast to the landed class's preference for the older and slower deed system with its emphasis on local histories and custom, the registration system sought to pronounce the reality of the present: the 'estate is a legal concept that represents time in land for the purposes of private property . . . Whereas paper deeds prove the existence of *already existing* title, registration brings title into being: each registered title is new, manufactured and guaranteed by the registry' (Keenan, 2019: 150). Law regulates across and produces social and civil space, and it regulates across and produces social and civil time.

Time-standardisation performs the nomorhythmic function of synchronisation across scales. These (variable) scales exhibit a level of contingency dependent on given technical, cosmological, epistemological, sociological, and other constraints. In the previous chapter, we considered Plato's attempted synchronisation of the juridico-political system as one that reached "up" to cosmological order and "down" to institutions and the soul-body compounds of citizens via statecraft-soulcraft, in a choreographed citizenship in which the principle of rhythm was pedagogically central. While our contemporary social, political, cultural, and technical context is distinct, the ambitions of our own legal and political systems are no less extensive in their synchronising scope. What is sought today is global temporal juridico-political synchronisation pursued through time-measurement systems seeking attunement to atomic and cosmic rhythms, and in contemporary capitalist milieus, these systems become the vehicle through which our rhythms of everyday life are subordinated to technosocial rhythms. We will discuss this through an exploration of aspects of the history and present of time-standardisation, with particular focus on the UK and, to a lesser extent, the US. This history is one that occurs in the courtroom, but also in the factory, the public house, and in the servers of Google. Rhythmanalysis seeks to connect such processes to the concrete everyday, and in particular to the dynamic relationship among (to use our terminology) the biorhythmic, the cosmorhythmic, and the technosocial rhythmic. In this vein, we will conclude §14 with a reflection on working time in this context.

§14.1 Time-Standardisation

In this section, we separate our analysis under two broad headings. The first is the problem of the *synchronisation of the everyday and the clock*, and the second is the *synchronisation of the clock with time*. Turning to the former, time-standardisation produces new forms of synchronisation to clocks running on standardised forms of time, but this is not only about developments in *technical* evolution (obviously significant), but about how clocks and time-standardisation functioned as part of a broader *social* evolution through which synchronisation to the clock has meant the subordination of everyday life to the juridico-political and economic obligations and competitive demands of liberal capitalist milieus.

Let us put ourselves into the context of a defendant in 1858 who, faced with ejectment, rushed to the court in Dorchester where one of the quarter-annual court of assize sittings were taking place. His hearing was scheduled for 10 am. He checked the town clock: it was before 10; he was safe. Upon meeting counsel in "advance", however, he discovered that his case had already finished before it was due to begin: the judge had already directed his verdict for the claimant. The defendant was (as far as the judge was concerned) late. The judge had been waiting, the claimant's counsel had been waiting, the jury had been waiting.

Such a scenario broadly describes the curious facts that occurred in *Curtis v. March* (1858). How did this the lack of *synchronisation* between judge and defendant transpire? The judge had sat on the bench at 10 am *by the time of the court's clock*, which was synchronised with Greenwich Mean Time (GMT). The claimant had based his scheduling on local Dorchester time (i.e., by the town clock). The *town* clock and the *court* clock were misaligned by some minutes. Whereas local time is anchored predominantly to the sun, GMT is anchored, of course, by establishing Greenwich as the foundational meridian (i.e., a line of 0° longitude passing from the north to the south of the globe through Greenwich) of time-measurement. According to the *town* clock, the claimant arrived at 9:58 am. The differences between local times can be measured through longitudinal calculations (where 15 degrees of longitude equal a difference of one hour), but time-standardisation through GMT necessitated the abandonment of local times in everyday life and the establishment of new quotidian rhythms. At this point, GMT was not yet the centralised measure of time by law. It was held subsequent to this juridico-temporal confusion that the 'time appointed for the sitting of a Court must be understood as the mean time at the place where the Court sits, and not Greenwich time, unless it be so expressed'.

In other words, following *Curtis*, the presumption was that court sitting times were expressed as local mean time rather than GMT. (Also of note is that the defendant was granted a new trial so that the case could be heard [Dyson, 1916: 467–468].) As was also the case in some later US cases – such as the 1889 Georgia court case of *Henderson v Reynolds*, where solar time was preferred to the "artificial" and "arbitrary" nature of railroad time, or raised in litigation where the *Curtis* decision formed a 'progenitor of a line of court decisions in the United States debating the appropriate means of telling time' (Parrish, 2002: 4; but also see Birth, 2019: 203) – common law courts were hesitant to adopt time-standardisation, even where courthouses themselves used GMT. In *Curtis*, Judge Frederick Pollock of the Court of Exchequer noted in *obiter* comments that a 'person hearing that the Court would sit at 10 o'clock would *naturally understand* that to mean 10 o'clock by the time of the place, unless the contrary was expressed' (para. 868, emphasis added). The very possibility of claiming local time as what would have been 'naturally' assumed highlights the contested nature of what counts as time and the changing nature of what counts as natural, proper, and normatively appropriate. Local mean time, at variation with GMT, was here expressed as the standard temporal anchor of synchronisation for everyday life.

David Rooney and James Nye's research into the adoption of standard time in the UK is a useful antidote to accounts which tell an all-too-simplistic and linear story where the forces of railroad and telegraph networks instituted time-standardisation without friction. They discuss a number of examples of temporal misalignment (including *Curtis*), with particular focus on industrial working conditions and licensing hours temporally limiting alcohol consumption. The latter of these was the object of juridico-political obsession, with 31 statutes concerning liquor sale and regulation between 1828 and 1889, a number of which limited the sale of alcohol by time (Rooney and Nye, 2009: 17; Paterson, 1894: ix–x). Likewise, this period saw successive forms of legislation concerning working conditions (e.g., The Factory Acts of 1802, 1831, and 1833) in which working hours were subject to new regulations regarding record-keeping and time-limitations (e.g., requiring records of time worked to be kept or limiting working days to ten hours, as with the 1847 Act). The 1844 Act provided that the working hours of children and young persons were to be regulated by 'a public clock, or by some other clock open to public view', which needed the approval of the district factory inspector (Rooney and Nye, 2009: 14). One of the key problems with the regulation concerning alcohol sale, as with the measuring of working days, was the question of *what* standard of measurement needed to be used. It was well documented (Thomas, 1948: 39, cited in Rooney and Nye, 2009: 14) that employers regularly kept two sets of clocks, one visible to workers and one not, by which they could extract free labour from workers beyond the legal limits. For laws concerning alcohol sale, these acts in fact did not specify *whose* clock publicans should refer to concerning closing time.

It was not until the *Statutes (Definition of Time) Act 1880* that such issues were addressed in statutory form, fixing the meaning of the word "time" as GMT in Britain and Dublin Mean Time in Ireland, which was 25 minutes and 21 seconds behind GMT. (Dublin time would be synchronised with GMT 36 years later via the *Time [Ireland] Act 1916*.) Subsequent acts (such as the *Summer Time Acts 1916* and then *1972*) established biannual variations in these timescapes for the putative goal of daylight saving (see Heaney, 2022).

Court time, pub time, and working time were thus three further key sites or tension points through which social, political, economic, and juridical forces interacted to produce standardised time and form the adoption of new rhythms of everyday life. Of course, the story of time's standardisation is impossible to tell at the domestic level alone. Time-keeping, time-standardisation, and time-management have been crucial in the history of imperialism, colonialism, empire, and (relatedly) the development of international institutions. This was gestured towards in §1 when we mentioned the British time-signal by cannon fire in South Africa's Cape of Good Hope. Discussing this, Rooney highlights how the British government's astronomers would provide accurate time-signals to ships when they ported, which would then be synchronised with shipboard chronometers, providing a reference through which longitude could be calculated whilst at sea (see Sobel, 2011). This allowed for reliable navigation, highlighting the interrelation between the navigation of space with the measurement, monitoring, and management of time. One is not stretching the facts to say, as Rooney does, that 'time signals and chronometers kept empires afloat' (2021: 102): ports functioned as *localities of synchronisation* in the resetting and repetition of those rhythms of colonial rule imposed by British political, administrative, judicial, and military forces. As argued by Geoff Gordon, the story of standardised time is also a story of transnational law in which the two are in a relationship of dynamic co-constitution: the development of standardised time was developed in particular jurisdictions, but it ultimately required a transjurisdictional approach to time measurement and regulation. Likewise, the development of transnational law was shaped by how time became the object of concern for transnational actors (industrial capitalists, international lawyers, politicians, and so on). Gordon's timeline of time-standardisation in international law (2018: 390–394) begins with the mail coach service of the British Post Office adopting and synchronising its clocks with GMT in 1784. The timeline continues through the key point 100 years later when Greenwich became the "prime meridian" following the International Meridian Conference in Washington, DC, and then the US passed the *Standard Time Act 1918*.

However, the story of time is not over. In the technorhythmic transition from analogue to digital technologies, new problems of precision and synchronisation emerged. The *speed* of such transactions requires ever more and more precise time-keeping systems. Whereas, in the late 19th century, the London Stock Exchange subscribed to the Standard Time Company's time-signal service, which was provided over electric telegraph wires, today's high-frequency trading markets require precision far beyond the technical capabilities of that period. It is useful to quote Rooney again here (2021: 77) to illustrate the temporal precision and depth to which our contemporary markets reach in the service of synchronisation. (Note that UTC refers to Coordinated Universal Time, the current primary time-standard, although GMT and UTC are now synchronised.)

> The European directive on markets in financial instruments which came into force in January 2018, known as MiFID II, selected UTC as its timescale, and demands time stamps precise to one second for human trades, or one-thousandth of a second for normal computer algo trades. But for HFT trades the time stamp must not deviate from true UTC by more than 100 microseconds, or millionths of a second, and it needs to have a precision – the gap between two successive stamps – of no more than one-millionth of a second. . . . MiFID II-compliant clocks stamp a million times each second. And those time stamps need to be found on every chip in every computer server in every trading exchange across the entire European financial market. . . . All the computers that are involved with financial trading across the whole of Europe need to show the same time as each other to *100 millionths of a second*. There are thousands upon thousands of such computers in a single data centre alone.

This technical evolution of ever-more precision and depth of temporal reach and measurement raises the second broad heading of this section. The first, recall, concerned the synchronisation of the everyday and the clock. The second concerns the *synchronisation of the clock with time*. This is the question of what it is that is being measured whenever clocks measure. Current developments in this area highlight that the story of time-standardisation is not yet over and that it remains an ongoing contested juridico-political field.

To explore this, we need to consider some of the details of UTC as civil timescale. The International Bureau of Weights and Measures (BIPM) produces UTC through compilation and calculation. The technical basis for UTC is International Atomic Time (TAI). BIPM calculates UTC through a weighted algorithm from about 500 (as of 2017) atomic clocks and takes the measurements of atomic clocks measuring *Système International d'unités* (SI) seconds. Atomic clocks since the second half of the 20th century onwards have progressed from keeping time to an accuracy of one second in 300,000 years in 1955 to today's atomic clocks which keep time to an accuracy of one second in 158 million years (Rooney, 2021: 78–79), and this progress towards ever-greater precision over vaster historical stretches of time does not appear to be slowing. Atomic clocks will measure some chosen vibrational and periodic frequencies of the activity of atoms. So, for example, the SI second is based on caesium-133 and measures its transition between energy states as the atoms are passed through a microwave field. BIPM defines the second technically as 'the duration of 9 192 631 770 periods of the radiation corresponding to the transition between the two hyperfine levels of the unperturbed ground state of the [caesium-133] atom' (BIPM, 2019).

However, UTC is not solely based on these atomic clocks, as it at present must be kept within 0.9 seconds of UT-1, a "Universal Time" measure of astronomical time or of Earth's rotation in space. Atomic clocks have a hyper-accuracy that measures the second in the process described previously in a *continuous* timescale, independent of Earth's rotation (Chester, 2015). In a phrase, TAI is synchronised to the atom (with a high degree of precision), whereas UT-1 is synchronised to the Earth (whose patterns of repetition are more irregular, but whose rotation is gradually slowing on average). UTC accounts for this misalignment between TAI and UT-1. UTC is a *discontinuous* timescale in that it is adjusted for the purposes of synchronisation through the insertion of leap seconds. UTC is thus an attempted synchronisation of atomic and cosmic time for the purposes of juridico-political synchronisation. Gary Genosko and Paul Hegarty have recently discussed this problem of the leap second as a contemporary site of corporate, technical, and political struggle:

> Due to the slowing of the Earth's rotation and hangover (a few milliseconds) of the length of a diurnal day just beyond 24h, UTC is behind the hyper-accuracy and stability of the mean time of hundreds of atomic clocks located around the world. The programmed insertion of compensatory time on New Year's Eve of 2016 marked the 27th occasion on which such positivity was required. It may not be the final one. There is now a difference of – 37s between UTC and TAI, or 27 insertions beyond the original difference of 10s.
>
> (2020: 1010)

The functioning of networked computing works best through continuous timescales. Since UTC is discontinuous due to the ongoing need for corrections via the leap second, such networks require irregular patches whenever leap seconds are announced to maintain the temporal continuity of network time, absent which, as Kevin Birth notes, 'computer networks crash as they send and receive unexpected timestamps' (2019: 205). The synchronisation of the clock with time is thus a problem whose transformation depends not only on scientific standards and technical capabilities, but also social demand. There are different approaches to resolving the problem of the leap second produced by this misalignment between cosmorhythms and the technical programs which order social rhythms. Google has its so-called *smearing* protocol which distributes the leap second across a 24-hour period and which it deploys in its Network Time Protocol servers (the so-called leap smear, which the Japanese stock markets also deployed [Birth, 2019: 207]), as opposed to strategies that, as Genosko and Hegarty put it, condense the leap second into taking a one-second "hit", which has been the general approach adopted in how UTC has added leap seconds in the past. Genosko and Hegarty highlight how this points us towards the continued corporate role in the production and management of time, rendering visible again the continuing struggle over *whose* time should be "standardised" and "naturalised" in international and domestic legal forms. The temporal foundations of our networks of communication, transport, trade, and other services which structure our quotidian rhythms remain active objects of juridico-political contestation.

§14.2 Rhythm, Desynchronisation, and Temporal Autonomy

Lefebvre notes that the *everyday* is a 'mode of administering society' (1988: 80); Mohamed Zayani describes it as an 'object of programming' (1999: 3); the rhythms, repetitions, and sequences of our quotidian activities are the infinitesimal targets of such administration and programming, of which time-standardisation is a crucial evolving element. Time-standardisation touches daily life as a social zeitgeber, structuring how we plan and manage our tasks into segmented time-slices, enabling precise synchronisation and navigation across time and space. Considering this history of time-standardisation rhythmanalytically, there are three points we wish to make.

First, time-standardisation is an ongoing, evolving technosocial process, not solely technically determined, and of juridico-political concern and significance. The establishment of Greenwich as the *prime* meridian was in many respects a contingent effect of empire. But the question of establishing a juridico-political solution to the problem of how to *measure* and *distribute* time remains an open one which from (at least) the railway to Google has attracted significant interest from capital. If we ought to have legal mechanisms in place for adjudicating on the proper measure of time, and the measurement processes as well as the effects of these mechanisms have pervasive effects on ordering and sequencing of our everyday lives, then it must be asked to what extent we can more forcefully treat this problem of the temporal measurement as a political and normative one. We will return to this point later.

Second, while time-standardisation's history (as with any history) comes with a large slice of contingency, it nonetheless serves a crucial nomorhythmic function: that of *synchronisation* and *co-ordination*. Time-standardisation and temporal regulations generally serve to produce civil time, but synchronisation and co-ordination do not mean simply (however significant this is) a shared agreement on the "now", but also an official past, as well as projections and commitments for the future. Time-standardisation is a response to the juridico-political problem of social synchronisation, and it enables the smooth *co-ordination* of the everyday. Co-ordination requires a shared reference point (the Sun, the clock), but additionally an agreed framework (legal, political, technical) upon which to decide what this shared reference point should be. Civil time legally *distributes* time in a territory and provides the context for *behavioural* co-operation. Civil time and calendars enable contractual mechanisms, labour relations, working time regulations, limited terms of office, reliable evidentiary chains, as well as functioning to enable planning and future-oriented commitments.

Co-ordination is temporally threefold as it concerns time-standardisation, producing a co-ordinated *past, present*, and *future*. The co-ordinated past is produced through the forming of *records* retaining an aligned historical account (think of the receipts of trade and their timestamps that might be required of a high-frequency trade, the title registration system, or the long-term effects of criminal records). The co-ordinated *present* is produced through a shared temporal anchor and the framework for that anchor, allowing quotidian scheduling to function reliably (enabling timely arrival at the court). The co-ordinated *future* is produced through protentional commitments, the entering into of obligations, shared calendars, legislative programs, and so on. Time measurement requires synchronisation with technical or natural objects, but this synchronisation is embedded with particular aesthetic frameworks, as Birth (2019: 199) notes:

> The currently dominant European timescale is a hodgepodge of ideas including the 24-hour day (an ancient Egyptian idea), the 60-minute hour and 60-second minute (a Babylonian idea), the decriminalized increments of less than a second (an inheritance from the French Revolution), the Roman calendar adjusted by a pope, the use of leap years and leap seconds to keep it all reconciled with the foibles of Earth's rotation and orbit.

From a rhythmanalytical perspective, one must expect that technosocial forces would operate through the administration and programming of everyday life (time-standardisation being but one such one modality of this), given our focus on the power and binding force of cycles and repetitions. What temporal frameworks are instituted and rhythmised into bodies will recursively impact the cycles and rhythms of the milieu, producing effects on the cosmorhythms, biorhythms, and technosocial rhythms that conditioned them in the first place.

Repetition is the tool of power; but sampling, as we have noted previously, is also a technique of creation. If time-standardisation functions to synchronise us with the technosocial rhythms of capital, one can imagine projects of creative desynchronisation where new forms of co-ordination are produced. An obvious example of such projects of creative desynchronisation would be the relationship between cosmorhythms and the technosocial rhythms of hyper-industrial capitalism (within which, broadly speaking, time-standardisation functions). Global systems of capitalist and hyper-industrialist extraction, production, consumption, light-speed communication, and speculation are *misaligned* with the cosmorhythmic foundations upon which our continued existence is based. Our global systems of time-synchronisation are absolutely crucial to this project of temporal misalignment. To this extent we can say that contemporary time-standardisation produces a *form* of synchronisation and co-ordination, but that it is in many respects in the service of a vast *arrhythmia* further misaligning our technosocial and cosmorhythms to the point of collapse.

A rhythmanalytical approach motivates us to consider how temporal technics can be learned and developed in the service of juridico-political experiments to create new modalities of technosocial synchronisation with our cosmorhythmic conditions. If indeed some form of *synchronisation* and *co-ordination* are necessary for the existence of any enduring technosocial milieu, then it is vital to develop frameworks which can creatively desynchronise our everyday life from the (hyper-industrial) arrhythmia we are caught within. Such work could explore how to embed intergenerational responsibility, ecological and geologic timescapes, as well as *temporal autonomy* (to which we turn in the next paragraph) into our forms of temporal synchronisation.

Third, as we saw above, part of the history of time-standardisation is entangled with that of factory and workplace regulations, limiting the legal use of an employee's time by employers, regulating the visibility of clocks in the workplace and standards that such clocks needed to be based on, and so forth. Workplace regulations occur at the intersection of the everyday life of the worker, their bio-rhythms, and the technosocial rhythms that program and order sonic and kinetic movements, gestures, and speed. We already highlighted (§4.1) how research in biological rhythm has explored how night-shift work disrupts circadian rhythms, reducing cognitive function, amongst other effects. Time-standardisation produces an official civil time and temporal framework for the operation of quotidian capitalist life (e.g., licensing laws, curfews, and employment contracts). This, on the one hand, orders and limits our movements through the legal space; and on the other, it has resulted in the creation and assertion of temporal limitations, for example, with reference to the biorhythmic limit of bodies.

Regarding such limits, although relatively rarely discussed or taken seriously, there is of course Article 24 of the Universal Declaration of Human Rights (UDHR), which in full says that 'everyone has the right to rest and leisure, including reasonable limitation of working hours and periodic holidays with pay'. This should be read in conjunction with Article 23, as together the two articles affirm just working conditions, 'non-discrimination in work, fair remuneration, as well as rights to unionise, to rest and leisure' (O'Connell, 2012: 179). Relatedly, there is the European Union's *Working Time Directive* (WTD). Implemented in the UK via the *Working Time Regulations* (WTR) *1998* by the then-Labour government, WTR introduced for the first time a range of employment provisions. The regulations provide for a statutory limit on average weekly hours of work (48 hours a week being the maximum for those over 18), periods of daily rest/breaks, limitations on the gaps between working days, annual leave entitlements, average days off per week, and controls on night-shift work, amongst others. Interestingly, the UK was the only then-EU member to implement this directive *with* the inclusion of a clause that allows employers to ask employees to opt out of the maximum hours worked per week (Blair et al., 2001: 41). The success of the directive is at best mixed (Nowak, 2018: 127–128).

What we would like to draw attention to here is how, when this framework of civil time is filtered into questions of fair and just working conditions in law, the framework leads to an impoverished vision of everyday life, which enforces rather than interprets how the biorhythms of the worker are continuously subordinated to the demands of (24/7 hyper-industrial; also see Rose, 2018) technosocial rhythms. Consider how the Courts of Justice of the EU (CJEU) understand the meaning of *working time* in WTD. As Rebecca Zahn (2021: 122–123) discusses (focusing on the two recent CJEU judgments of *DJ v Radiotelevizija Slovenija* and *RJ v Stadt Offenbach am Main*), WTD is interpreted by CJEU in terms of that which gives legal form to art. 31(2) of the EU's Charter of Fundamental Rights. To quote Article 31 in full:

Article 31 – Fair and just working conditions
    1. Every worker has the right to working conditions which respect his or her health, safety and dignity.
    2. Every worker has the right to limitation of maximum working hours, to daily and weekly rest periods and to an annual period of paid leave.

In Article 31, and in CJEU's understanding of working time exhibited in the case law, a connection is drawn between working conditions which are healthy, safe, and respect worker dignity, with temporal limitations across quotidian, weekly, and annual cycles. These cases examine whether and how "standby" time at home could be understood as "working time" to trigger WTD. CJEU determined it could be applied whenever a worker is 'constrained *objectively and very significantly* in their ability to manage their free time when their professional services are not required' (Zahn, 2021: 123) when on standby. WTD defines working time as 'any period during which the worker is working, at the employer's disposal and carrying out his activity or duties' (art. 2[1]) and rest time as any time that is not working time (art. 2[2]).

In contemporary liberal capitalist milieus, work time and rest time, or more specifically labour and leisure, are produced as a legal binary which are temporally and juridically exclusive, giving rise to extensive case law such as this in the inevitable grey area that emerges when such binaries are legally imposed. As Julie L. Rose notes (2016: 34), such a conception of leisure as the simple inverse of labour is by far the most common in approaches to leisure in liberal legal and political theory, mentioning John Rawls (1993: 173–211) and Ronald Dworkin (2002) specifically. Leisure time is conceived as something that is *purchased* (either through the spending of income or the opportunity cost of lost earnings) as well as subject to choice and preference. Labour time *or* leisure time is the fundamental temporal trade-off for the liberal-capitalist individual. Their judgment on these trade-offs is a matter of *preference* upon which two reasonable people could disagree due to, for example, how differing views on the good life mean different time-usage preferences. The conception of civil time at play here, produced and enforced by legal and political institutions, is one of metricised linear and divisible time, anchored in those techniques of time-measurement and time-standardisation discussed previously. While some limited recognition is given to the right to rest and leisure for reasons of bio-rhythmic necessity and to alleviate the appearance of exploitation, by continually reinforcing and reproducing linear-divisible time as the metric of operation for everyday life, our frameworks of legal and civil time produce impoverished visions of rest and of time spent not selling labour time.

In other words, as important as the gains in working time limitations have been and from which there is scope to extend much further, the linear and metric juridico-political framework of time in which everyday life is formed colonises everyday life into a binary of labour and leisure: labour being the time-slices where supply is governed, and leisure being the time-slices where demand is governed. Everyday life thereby becomes the temporal sequencing and ordering (the rhythm) of supply and demand. Recall that, in §5.1, we noted the distinction between *cyclical* and *linear* time in Lefebvre and Régulier's rhythmanalytical research. The abstract, quantitative, homogeneous clock time of time-standardisation cuts time into equally manageable, fragmented, and discrete slices. Technosocial rhythms in capitalist milieus tend to mobilise and measure time as a linear phenomenon: labour extracted from workers is measured and remunerated on the basis of time-measurement, where what is measured are discrete and homogenous time-slices or units. Lefebvre and Régulier highlight the tension between linear and cyclical time as in a constant struggle over the use and deployment of time. They consider how it is in the cyclic quality of rhythm that replenishment, renewal, and rest function: rest describes those cycles which require attention for biorhythmic, psychic, and social replenishment. While rhythm can be subject to abstraction and formal and metrified measurement, it nonetheless resists total capture by it. The time of everyday life – the times of work, play, rest, desire, and need, as their dynamic interactions – is never fully incorporated or captured by the deadening scripts of linear time and the mutual disjunction between labour and leisure it reproduces. Through mechanisms such as WTD, by locking questions of rest and work into this disjunctive binary within a linear framework, the EU and CJEU perpetually reinforce an impoverished image of time whereby rest and associated rhythms are packaged into a legal form which subjects it to temporal scheduling and metric control. By slicing up time into pieces and placing it on a work-rest binary, everyday life remains within the perpetual orbit of labour for workers. From a rhythmanalytical perspective, the cyclic rhythms of rest which are of such biorhythmic, psychic, and social significance operate in a different modality of temporality and are thus ignored through the reproduction of a temporal framework which obsessively scripts the everyday into such apparently discrete slices of labour and leisure. Less working time means, in fact, no rest: only shorter or longer breaks.

The distribution of civil time slices everyday life into units in ways that have become increasingly important for the recording of evidentiary chains for HFT transactions, for the smooth functioning of global digital infrastructures, and for the recording and measuring of working hours. WTD sets legal-regulatory limits in the nomological distribution of labour and leisure within the framework of temporal, linear, and sliced standardised time. While longer breaks are preferable to no breaks, for the rhythmanalyst, the entire temporal framework at play and the ways this framework is reproduced in its everyday enforcement here serves primarily to divorce us from any potential of *temporal autonomy*. If temporal autonomy is to mean anything – and such a concept will require a much deeper consideration than we can give briefly here – it must relate the time of everyday life and how it is distributed, while remaining as much as possible *open to determination* by those in the milieu; or, to put this differently, temporal autonomy in one's rhythms of everyday life requires it to be effectively the case that one can determine one's own protentional trajectories. Linear time is formally determined, even if its content can be "filled" with different forms of content (labour or leisure), through which the role of the worker is to fill this preset script in the most efficient and "preferable" manner.

The question of the right to free time concerns the politics of time-measurement and the processes through which legal, political, economic, and social institutions synchronise and co-ordinate us in time and space. These shape the aesthetic character of our rhythms of everyday life. The arrhythmia between the *cyclical* and the *linear* is in this sense both the most abstract and the most concrete, whether it is in exhaustion or burnout from subordinating one's biorhythms to the demands of technosocial rhythms (through long hours or shift work), the inevitable tension that emerges between the temporal demands and obligations of the employment contract and the actual patterns of life which disrupt our ability to fulfil these obligations, or how the "flexible" worker becomes legally obligated to sacrifice their time-slices with the promise of consistent labour and payment remaining non-guaranteed. While the linear framework which makes a binary distinction between work and non-work (leisure) is chosen based on individual preferences, Lefebvre cautions us about drawing too sharp a distinction between that which is done of necessity and that which is done of desire. He notes (Lefebvre, 2013: 26): 'Between need and desire there is a well-known difference, but there is no discontinuity.... Need and desire, sleep and wake, work and repose are rhythms in interaction.' These juridico-political temporal frameworks are not only conceptually insufficient in their capturing of the qualitative and temporal character of everyday life, but they also lock the everyday in an arrhythmic struggle in which contemporary liberal capitalist milieus appear unable to dislodge themselves. Building on this, we suggest that rhythmanalysts should concern themselves with the study and creation of, as well as experimentation with, frameworks of temporal autonomy at the level of everyday life. Temporal autonomy, whereby one's rhythms of everyday life can become open to determination rather than rigidly scheduled, scripted, and controlled, is a problem that the rhythmanalyst must confront. This confrontation must be taken into the theoretical and practical domains of social, civil, and legal arrangements to create new forms of co-ordination and synchronisation.

§14.3 Refrain

In this section, we have sought to highlight the purchase of rhythm to law via the question of time-standardisation, a process through which our motions are ordered, synchronised, and co-ordinated, with reference to planetary and atomic (via UTC) time, beating to the technosocial rhythms of hyper-industrial capital. This juridico-political context linearises the form of temporality we are more or less obligated to relate to and participate in for everyday life. We have tried to indicate that, to the extent that technosocial forces shape civil time in a manner which puts our practices in an arrhythmic relationship with our cosmological and ecological conditions, we are invited to explore modes of *desynchronisation* and new forms of *synchronisation*, not just at the level of everyday life (via temporal autonomy), but in how our time-measurement systems embed (or do not embed) our rhythmic entanglement with previous and future generations as well as our ecological and cosmological contexts.

§15 The Temporalities of Lawmaking and the Contraction of Juridico-Political Continuity

Temporality is often part of the *unthought* of legal theory and practice. The question of time is thought to be separate, for example, in jurisprudential debates on the nature, purpose, and function of law. Law is often implicitly imagined as external to or unrelated to time (as when law is imagined as determined by some ahistorical idea of reason). It is imagined as part of the "natural" order – under, upon, or contained within which the *artifice* of law operates – or assumed as the necessary anchor through which social synchronisation and co-ordination can function. Practitioners, for their part, tend to need to know what time *it* is and *which* legal time pertains, not what *time* is. But it is not so easy for us to separate ourselves from time: law cannot be dissociated from the organisation and distribution of time, those mechanisms of measurement, synchronisation, and co-ordination which permeate and aesthetically order our everyday lives. Law records and remembers, follows us in time, both constraining some and enabling other protentional trajectories in everyday life. Law is in the business of producing, organising, and enforcing time, rhythmising and putting into play expectation frameworks.

The key aim of this section is to explore how more detailed inclusion of law as a domain with its own durations, patterns, and motifs can enrich rhythmanalytical research and critique. With important exceptions (Novak, 2017; Dakka and Davitti, 2022), little work has been done at this intersection and more rhythmanalyses, we will argue, need to explore the ways in which legal institutions and practices are central to production, reproduction, and transformation of the everyday. While it does not exhaust his position, Lefebvre, for example (2014: 798) in Volume III of his *Critique*, situates law, regulations and prohibitions alongside apparatuses of justice as, respectively, direct and indirect forms through which *the state* 'manages daily life'. While their dynamic interactions are continuous and, in many cases, understated, we reject the extent to which such a position displays a tendency to *reduce* the juridical to the political in our rhythmanalysis of everyday life. Simple forms of such subordination come with three problems. First, such a reduction tends to elide the complexity of law's role in everyday life across historical stretches. Second, by paying less independent attention to interactions between law and time, rhythmanalysts have done less work on specific nomorhythmic objects: from particular laws and regulations, to rituals and practices, to transformations in legal systems through, for example, the introduction of new technologies (see Kwapińska, 2022), all of which remain open for future researchers to explore. Third, rhythmanalysis has yet to deeply explore the critical potentials that could be experimented with in everyday life through the creation of new legal frameworks and rituals.

No doubt, judicial power is in many respects politically produced, for example, in how the existence of courts in contemporary liberal capitalist milieus (and especially appellate courts) rely upon some hierarchical organisation of powers which cannot ultimately be separated from political power. We are used to thinking about legal and political authority in terms of space and territory: the *jurisdiction* of courts is, for example, significantly related to the boundaries of political authorities. But for the rhythmanalyst, legal institutions and practices need to be approached through how they produce the space-times of the milieu. Legal authority will not only have spatial extension and limitations, but also temporal ones, and embed within them certain narratives which temporalise its legitimation with reference to histories and futures such that the legal framework of everyday life enlists our participation therein.

Building on this, our focus is on quotidian roles of judicial and law-enforcing institutions, in interaction with overtly political institutions and practices, in consolidating what we are calling the *contraction of juridico-political continuity* of a milieu (or sometimes the establishment of *legal duration*). Law orders the movements (rhythms) of the milieu in everyday life, structuring the *temporal continuity* of the milieu and (re-)producing it in everyday life, producing and managing the past, present, and future of the milieu. In order to develop a clearer sense of what we mean by this term, let us first consider *contraction*. Contraction names, for example, that process through which the lived experience of duration is *held* or *bound* together in the appearance of continuity: the *passive* and *habitual* process through which, when hearing the looping rhythm of a song, it is in experience synthesised into a living present in which *expectations* are generated about what is to come. The contraction of experienced temporal continuity is attached to expectation frameworks and the stabilisation of experience. Without contraction and its stable expectation frameworks (e.g., if there is some entrance of the *unexpected* into the temporal flow of experience), there is at least the *threat* of insecurity unless that unexpected element is then subsequently integrated and consolidated. This integration itself would be a process of contraction through which the unexpected is incorporated into the temporal flow, producing a newly configured temporal continuity.

Beyond simply the level of the contraction of the temporal continuity of individual experience, the contraction of juridico-political continuity consists in those habits and rituals at the level of the *milieu* through which we generate a relatively synchronised social space held together by institutional practices (e.g., juridical, political, and economic). Of course, we cannot *totally* divorce the contraction of temporal experience from the contraction of juridico-political continuity, since the former will often include those *legal* expectation frameworks that one has learned and habitually come to anticipate. Contraction at the level of experience cuts across past, present, and future, involving and invoking memory to structure the present and always producing and configuring future expectations. Juridico-political contraction, too, cuts across these three temporal flows:

(1) Regarding the "past" or the *retentional* element of juridico-political continuity: the authority of legal rules and practices will generally (continually re-) produce or rely upon some sense of history or of the past as its ground of legitimation – one cannot be prosecuted for crimes that do not yet exist, and so all criminal prosecution must be grounded in some law that defined and criminalised some act in the past.

(2) Regarding the "present" or *attentional* element of juridico-political continuity: everyday life is lived as the choreography of one's sonic and kinetic motions in relation to that legal architecture, comprising sequences of repetition (adherence to participation

in embedded rituals, customs, and norms) and improvisations of difference (whenever one is confronted with a "new" context to respond to). Roberts (2013: 17–18) discusses how any social grouping, if it is to endure, must resolve the double problem of how to establish order (continuity, repetition) in everyday life as well as how to respond to disorder (discontinuity, difference) such that both can be integrated into a generally shared set of expectation frameworks. Law comprises this set of expectations of everyday behaviour but also those expectations about procedures when the unexpected occurs (via, e.g., rituals of dispute resolution). Although we will not discuss it in any further detail in this chapter, we discussed in §6 Orr's work on rhythm and electoral cycles, such that we can see how the legal and political recursively interact in liberal capitalist societies through elections as a resolution to the problem of *succession* (a perennial problem of discontinuity in any milieu). Aside from the problem of succession, juridico-political institutions and practices also face the problem of establishing ordered conduct in everyday life (obedience, the proper choreography of sonic and kinetic motions) and in responding to problems of disorder (through violent law enforcement, punishment, dispute resolution, and so forth).

(3) Regarding the "future" or the *protentional* element of juridico-political continuity, expectation frameworks are stabilised and modes of planning made possible through law. The entrance of a new law which defines and criminalises some conduct will require legal subjects to adjust their future behaviour as well as their future expectations about the behaviour of others; entering into a contract will commit oneself and others into some future obligations, usually with time-specified deadlines for fulfilment.

Although these are not the only temporal configurations law can take, law tends to mobilise and configure the past, present, and future of the milieu in its attempt to manage order and disorder towards the contraction of *juridico-political continuity*.

Building on these initial comments, this section will now devote itself to the second central purpose of this chapter: articulating the relevance *of* law *to* rhythm. We will explore what we noted previously, namely the complexity of law's role in the establishment of juridico-political continuity across long stretches of time through a discussion of the relationship and temporal distinctions between common law and statutes. Against any total reduction of the juridical to the political, we instead will speculate upon the relationship between common law and statute in terms of different speeds and slownesses, which interact to integrate law into the milieu. For reasons we will explore, the operation of statute law tends to have immediate and instant protentional force: an automatically authoritative act. Statute law has this character of *rapid* normativity. Common law – and again we are speaking in tendencies – operates on a different temporal register. The protentional force of common law is historically weighty, and its normative force is of a *slower* form. The dynamic interactions of these *rapid* and *slow* normative forces – as distinct "sources" of law – give form to law in everyday life, establishing a temporal horizon of juridico-political continuity for the milieu. We will first explore statute law (§15.1), then common law (§15.2), and will then conclude this chapter with some speculations and reflections on their interactions (§15.3).

§15.1 Lex Scripta

Matthew Hale, in his *History of the Common Law of England*, famously structured his investigation via an opening conceptual and juridical division between *Lex Scripta* (the written law) and *Lex non Scripta* (unwritten law). The former pertains primarily to statute law. The legitimate production of statute law follows an aesthetic and temporal composition through which law is contracted into orthographic form and, when coupled with the consent of the House of Commons, the House of Lords, and the monarch, becomes *posited* law. This process of consent-acquisition occurs in ordered steps (as, today, via the distinct stages of the first reading, second reading, committee, report, third reading, potential amendments, and the legislative dance this can ignite between the House of Commons and the House of Lords) as an institutional procedure for establishing simultaneity of consent prior to the written word being marked with the stamp of posited law. This ritual of lawmaking, combining orthographic and choreographic arrangements, establishes formal procedures and rites through which what becomes recorded is not simply the written law, but written law marked by its passage through the ritual of lawmaking.

Thomas Hobbes, in his late *Dialogue Between a Philosopher and a Student, of the Common Laws of England*, argues that the reason of the monarch, 'when it is publickly upon Advice, and Deliberation declar'd, is that *Anima Legis*, and that *Summa Ratio*, and that Equity which all agree to be the Law of Reason, is all that is, or ever was Law in *England*, since it became Christian, besides the Bible' (2008: 19). *Anima legis* is the soul or spirit of the law – its principle of movement or that which grounds law's binding force – which, for Hobbes, is marked by the authoritative sign of sovereignty. Written law, properly composed via its ordered institutional routes and routines (e.g., today, via procedures of democratic deliberation), has a more or less *automatic* or *instant* legal legitimacy or authority. This is partly why Hobbes (1996: 184) can argue that a law that has been in use for a considerable period has *no* binding force *due* to this temporal stretching: 'it is not the Length of Time that maketh the Authority, but the Will of the Soveraign signified by his silence', such that the silence of the sovereign on custom or tradition grants legal authority more powerfully than custom or tradition itself. Against the common law view (of which Edward Coke is taken as the example by Hobbes), whereby law's binding force is tied in some significant sense to custom and to the related historically developed *artificial reason* of the courts as considered and deliberated upon by judge, Hobbes rejects that law's authority can be so founded on some anchor (custom, precedent) in deep social time. In 1897, Oliver Wendell Holmes Jr. (1995: 399) famously rearticulated a version of this:

> It is revolting to have no better reason for a rule of law than that so it was laid down in the time of Henry IV. It is still more revolting if the grounds upon which it was laid down have vanished long since, and the rule simply persists from blind imitation of the past.

Hobbes rejects the previously mentioned distinction between natural and artificial reason relied upon in common law theory (CLT). Broadly construed, the judge in CLT is taken to have privileged access to this artificial reason and historically developed sense of the customs of a milieu, precedent, and ability to determine what is a legally, institutionally, and (perhaps) morally appropriate decision to be made in the particulars of a given case. Related to this rejection, Hobbes thereby also rejects that this (historically developed and temporally dense) notion of judicial wisdom (through precedent and artificial reason) provides judicial access to lawmaking, for it 'is not Wisdom, but Authority that makes a Law' (2008: 10). Law is not produced by the courts, but by that juridico-political ritual of lawmaking by the 'Kings of *England*, consulting with the Nobility and Commons in *Parliament*' (2008: 10).

Taking these combined considerations of both Hale and Hobbes with respect to *Lex Scripta*, we can note the following. The composition of written law is a ritual of legislative endurance, comprising orthographic reduction and continuous change as the proposed law proceeds through ritual institutional passages prior to the establishment of simultaneous legislative consent effectively through formal procedures and the attainment of royal assent in the UK. Such processes can be slow. Indeed, while it is important not to overstate this, there is evidence to suggest that such lawmaking is slowed down in relation to increased transaction costs that can come alongside larger lawmaking bodies (such as the European Union) (Hertz and Leuffen, 2011; Toshkov, 2017). However, the production of written law by legislative bodies is not exactly non-productive. Tom Bingham, in his *Rule of Law*, complained of the UK Parliament's 'legislative hyperactivity' (2011: 40), highlighting how the continuous cycles through which written laws are produced poses challenges from a rule of law perspective, because such speed compresses the time of thought required for judges to assimilate and interpret law. On this point (and these broad numbers only give an indication), a briefing paper published by the House of Commons Library (Lightbown and Smith, 2009), for example, indicated a clear upward trend in pages of new written law, including acts and statutory instruments (SIs), over the period 1911–2006. To give some specifics, there were 2,880 pages in 1955; 6,070 pages in 1965; 8,270 pages in 1975; 7,140 pages in 1985; 12,690 pages in 1995; and 15,596 pages in 2005. The inclusion of SIs in this calculation is significant, as there is no clear upward trend in the number of *acts* passed and given that SIs tend to be passed with much less deliberative scrutiny (or active consent) as compared to acts. The measure of page numbers helps to account, additionally, for the changing length of acts. As such, there are grounds for suggesting that centralisation of lawmaking over large territories may slow lawmaking in some respects to the extent that it is constrained by juridico-political rituals, but it is undoubtedly the case that contemporary legislatures are veritable institutional machines which ceaselessly produce ever more law in increasing volume and speed. The slowing effect of ritual, in addition, can at times be streamlined. Although we will not discuss this in detail here, when in the context of a perceived emergency or in perceived exceptional circumstances, as Michael Foran (2021: 123–124) notes, one approach to such crises is that they can be said to transform the 'normative landscape' such that 'adherence to existing legal standards can frustrate measures designed to address the urgent concerns which led to this state of crisis in the first place.' Faced with threats to the juridico-political continuity of the milieu (threats to social order), the rituals of lawmaking are easily stripped down to attain an even faster intervention into everyday life. For example, this instant normativity and rapid choreographic transformation of the everyday in relation to emergency measures can be easily associated with those introduced in response to COVID-19 (Ağca-Varoğlu, 2021; De Wandeler et al., 2020) – but emergencies are by no means juridico-politically uncommon (Neocleous, 2006; De Wilde, 2015; Wallace, 2020; Coaffee, 2021).

The legitimate composition of written law will, in normal circumstances, step to these designated and paced institutional habits and routines as an ordered sequence of movements which constitute authoritative legal creation. The ritual of lawmaking is subject to continuous repetition in the making of new written law, such that authoritative lawmaking has to follow a particular ordered sequence of movements perpetually repeated in each re-enactment. As Margaret Davies notes (2017: 75), this can theoretically ground legal authority (in, e.g., legal positivism) in some *stable* (if not quite static) reference point, namely, some set of social facts regarding what is recognised as the authoritative procedure for lawmaking. ('Their argument is that legal authority does not move with time: rather, legal change is explained by an underlying reason or authority which is itself stable'.) Nonetheless, the repetition of these procedures are, of course, not mechanical and are themselves continuously changing through subtle developments in custom or legislative intervention as, for example, through the *Parliament Acts 1911* and *1949* which thereby limited the ability of the House of Lords to *delay* the lawmaking ritual in particular instances. The requirement, for example, for simultaneous consent between monarch, lords, and commons can be traced back to the early 15th century. In addition, it has been suggested that this consent requirement played an important role in the increased legislative scrutiny placed on the precise wording of bills and increased reliance on precision in the writing of law. Acts of Parliament have been printed upon their passing since 1484 (Baker, 2019: 218–219). If this is a stable reference point for authoritative lawmaking, this form must be understood as a *fluid form*, as a long-term juridico-political and nomogenetic dance which is anything but static.

The closure of the ritual marked by the attainment of consensus, writing, and royal assent marks the temporal completion of the passage of lawmaking, such that new law thereby opens onto a new temporal and juridico-political horizon which the ritual grounded: the future. new law has an instantaneity of authority. This does not mean that new acts are immediately applied across a territory after the "moment" of royal assent, but rather that the passage through royal assent constitutes the recorded mark of *posited* law having endured the ritual of lawmaking, automatically creating new protentional trajectories. For example, a new act may not become effective immediately but will often create new legal obligations and expectation frameworks with respect to which legal officials and subjects are choreographed. *Lex Scripta* is both retentional and protentional: it marks, records, and repeats the process through which the law was orthographically reduced, ritually approved, and thereby posited; but it also thereby protentionally shapes (though it does not determine) its effects, such as the processes through which that written law is enforced, applied, interpreted by courts, and so on. The temporality of *Lex Scripta* operates through constituting a particular relationship to the past and to the future. It rests upon and samples traditional and ritualised practices of lawmaking (orthography, choreography, simultaneous consent) in order to announce, declare, and create the new, and in such a way can simultaneously be thought of as both relying upon historical legitimation (through the performed re-enactment of the ritual lawmaking process) as well as denying the ultimate binding power of history as each new written law can, here speaking broadly, "make or unmake" any law, and Parliament cannot bind its successors (per *Ellen Street Estates v Minister of Health*).

Written law relies upon the past for its formal procedures of legitimation but simultaneously places normative authority in the *present* in a double movement which grounds and ungrounds the law's relationship to the past. The making of written law comprises that rhythmic play of difference, repetition, and judgment we have met on a number of occasions: if the act of positing new law in the present can be considered as a moment of collective judgment, this positing must be supported by the repetition of the appropriate ritual, binding it to the past, such that it can shape the future. The past is bound to and hinged to the present and future for the attempted (re-)establishment of juridico-political continuity.

As Shirin M. Rai (2010: 288) notes, such ceremony and ritual in Parliament can be analysed on at least two levels. The first is through the 'casting of spectacles through which the formal-juridical power of the state is operationalised', which could draw our analytical attention to how the aesthetic overload of juridico-political ritual is in the service of its reproduction through ritualised repetition. The second is 'where bodies perform in space and time – as men, women, able and less able, black or white' (also see Coole, 2007), forcing us to consider the different modalities through which quotidian rhythms are distributed according to power relations of the milieu. A third level, which we would add, concerns how lawmaking is involved in the constitution of the temporality of juridico-political milieu across past, present, and future. It involves the *selection* of elements of the past *repeated* in the present (through formal repetition of the periodic components of lawmaking), posited as recorded and written law publicly declaring the collective judgment of lawmakers. This sampling of the past is attached to this positing and thereby creates future legal trajectory (enforcement, application, interpretation) in the constitution or contraction of juridico-political continuity. One of the significant features of this process from a temporal perspective is that it enables and makes possible discontinuities, potentially threatening to juridico-political continuity, to be integrated within legal duration. Legal institutions and practices – which are central in the framing of expectation frameworks – are themselves used to transform expectation frameworks when creating new law. Subject, for example, to contingency (difference) which threatens the milieu, the making of written law performs as an agent of rapid social choreography in the maintenance of juridico-political continuity.

Returning to Hale's distinction between written and unwritten law, it is of note that statute law itself rests upon a deeper temporal periodisation. On the one hand, there are those statutes or acts made since the accession of Richard I in 1189, defined as to be part of the time of *legal memory*, broadly considered as the official and ordered record of posited law. On the other hand, statutes made before this so-called *Time of Memory* are those which have become incorporated into the common law which, while lacking a temporally discrete point of origin (as opposed to the officially posited and recorded law of statutes within legal memory), have instead diffuse and deep temporal origins as indicated by terms such as custom, tradition, and "immemorial usage", which, practically speaking, can be considered as prior to 1189 (Davies, 2017: 48). The common law, to which we will turn in more detail, has a distinct dance and operates at a temporal asymmetry to statute law, but in a way that helps to facilitate and fasten the bonds of juridico-political continuity all the same. Statute law, as we have seen, has a limited ritual element which constrains its processes of legitimation and authorisation, but it is also a fast form of social normativity with a wide protentional scope. (Parliament can make or unmake any law.) Common law, in contrast, anchors itself in deeper temporal roots and operates through slower normative processes, and its openness to the future is generally partial, conservative, and cautious. While a full analysis of juridico-political continuity would incorporate an analysis of a more expanded range of institutions and practices (e.g., administrative agencies, police, and prisons), for our purposes the key relationship to consider is how statute law and the common law dynamically interact to (re-)produce the temporal integrity and continuity of the legal and political system. Once written law completes its passage towards the status of posited law, there is the more temporally diffuse and often disordered process through which the written law becomes incorporated (or not) after its activation and promulgation into the quotidian everyday life of legal officials and subjects. This in effect takes us away from the process of the making of written law towards the process through which that law interacts with the milieu more generally and how it is integrated into quotidian rhythms, obliging choreographed responses from, for example, the police, the courts, and legal subjects. We will now turn in more detail to the common law's role here in terms of how it conceives of the temporality of lawmaking and its role in the contraction of juridico-political continuity.

§15.2 Lex Non Scripta

As Postema discusses (1986: 5), broadly situating the development of classical CLT in the late 16th and early 17th centuries, CLT tends to identify its legitimacy and authority as a source of law and law-creation through 'general use and acceptance'. Such usage and acceptance point us towards two themes central for us: that of the *temporal* and that of the *quotidian*. Continued usage over time constitutes evidence of acceptance (which in CLT is a key marker of legal validity) such that those laws which have stood the so-called test of time have enhanced validity: their continued usage and acceptance constitute important evidence of the "reasonableness" of that custom or practice. The time of everyday life is, in CLT, a principle of legal validation and in itself is considered as a check on reasonableness: 'Only time can tell whether a rule becomes a law, because only time – i.e. practice and use over time – validates' (Postema, 1986: 5). The time of everyday life, including the everyday life of the courts in its interactions with the milieu, is the vital and continuing source of the authority of common law.

For the rhythmanalyst, what is *common* about the common law is less about a common *territory* over which the law spreads (such borders themselves being open and changing historical processes), the commonality of some particular *people* (such ideas of "peoples" being frozen and fictional snapshots of open and changing historical processes), or indeed even the commonality of the *laws* themselves (which must continuously change and be adapted in response to changing technosocial conditions, legislative programs, and so forth). Rather, common law is more about the precarious and continuous work of (re-)establishing a common *time* for the milieu (what we are calling juridico-political continuity). Given the openness and contingency of historical processes, the work of continually establishing and re-establishing the juridico-political continuity through which the milieu ties itself to this supposed deep quotidian and juridical past is a significant aspect of the work of the common law. Just as we are to an important extent bound to our biological and ecological histories, the patterns which structure everyday life (custom, tradition) for CLT are embedded so deep within the functioning of a milieu that they can be conceived of as (at least) a constitutive component of the common ground which binds those in a milieu to that past and to each other. Just as, to continue the loose comparison, our evolution as a species has produced an aesthetic framework for how we sense the world (such as the human hearing range), custom and tradition are considered in CLT in like manner as that which have become so historically embedded so as to have produced an aesthetic framework for how we perceive, understand, and interact with others in a given milieu. We can call this *common sense*, if by this we refer to that which can be (emotionally, affectively) perceived or (rationally) judged as, for example, "reasonable" or "unreasonable" by those acculturated to and embedded within the milieu. The common law is thus concerned every day with the establishment of juridico-political continuity through anchoring in the supposed deep past, and with the distribution, production, and reproduction of that historically evolved common sense of a milieu.

For Matthew Hale (1971: 17, quoted in Postema, 1986: 5), while laws are often written, their 'formal and obliging Force and Power . . . grows by long Custom and Use'. The temporality of everyday life is thus heavily weighted with history in the common law: historical ways of life, customs, practices, traditions, and so forth, which those in the milieu (whether consciously or not) re-enact, repeat, relegitimise, and often participate in the slow transformation thereof. The "American Blackstone" James Kent (1840: 343, quoted in Parker, 2011a: 1–2), echoing such a viewpoint, argued that the common law:

> Fills up every interstice, and occupies every wide space which the statute law cannot occupy. . . . [W]e live in the midst of the common

law, we inhale it at every breath, imbibe it at every pore; we meet with it when we wake, and when we lie down to sleep, when we travel and when we stay at home; and it is interwoven with the very idiom that we speak; and we cannot learn another system of laws, without learning, at the same time, another language.

Law is composed not simply – and not principally – in the artificial reason of written judgments, but at the level of the choreography of everyday life through which law is re-enacted, repeated, and relegitimised, whereby, to quote Postema (1986: 6, emphasis added):

> Public action, then, takes on a quasi-ritualistic character. It is a re-enactment of patterns known and recognized through time, *reaffirming the continuities binding members of this social partnership.*

Given the common law's coextensiveness with everyday life in this image, CLT will generally hesitate to associate the practice of the judge as a *lawmaking* one, thinking instead of the judicial decision-making process as one either through which the privileged epistemic gaze of the judge (as devoted student of the common law) can uncover its historical truth *or* through which the judge, as privileged ontological agent of the law, becomes that through which some embedded legal truth can be newly expressed (e.g., translated, adapted) in transformed social conditions. It is in fact in the rhythms of everyday life (which is to say the court's judgment thereof), tied and bound to the common time of the milieu, whereby the common law's truth, legitimacy, and feasibility are ultimately tested. On this view, time is less an empty container, than a repository of tradition, custom, and ritual (Postema, 1986: 5) subject to subtle change and variation, as well as continuity and repetition, in how we (and especially judges) as legal subjects relate to law in everyday life. Kent's comparison to language in the previous quote is useful on this point to the extent that it points towards how language is continually undergoing subtle change and variation through the evolution of linguistic practices, and it is not uncommon for the "official" adoption of such changes to be merely retrospectively rubber-stamping developments that have already occurred. CLT presented in this manner is thus a rich field for rhythmanalytical research which could investigate the historical and evolving relationship between the common law and everyday life, as well the more general and long-term rhythms of legal evolution through the common law.

The common law approach to the establishment of juridico-political continuity involves this important relationship to the deep past and custom, such that the normative speed of common law is cautious and more closed with respect to the future compared to the comparable openness and speed that statute law can exhibit. Whereas the creative power of statute law in the context of Parliamentary sovereignty is unmoored to and unbound by the past with respect to the content of new law (if not unrestrained by the forms and rituals to grant this new law authoritative status), CLT's purported deep historical roots function like an anchor both with regard to slowing the movement of the common law and constraining protentional trajectories thereby. Whereas posited law is within that which Hale calls the *Time of Memory* (namely, officially recorded memory, part of what is consciously sensed by legal institutions with a clear identifiable point of origin), common law instead is considered as being the historically sedimented customs and practices of the milieu for which no discrete origin point can be identified.

Custom – per John Davies's (quoted in Pocock, 1987: 32–33) *Irish Reports* as the-then attorney general for Ireland in the early 17th century – becomes law when that custom is continued and has not been interrupted within legal memory. Common law is described in this sense as *time out of mind*, which accounts for the law's legitimacy as pertaining to its location in deep social time, but it is also a speculative history which is anchored on the very *lack* of clear historical accounts. Hale (1971: 4) highlights that law '*before* Time of Memory is supposed without a Beginning, or at least such a Beginning as the Law takes Notice of' and such laws 'obtain their Strength by meer immemorial Usage or Custom'. Custom becomes law when the habit is so ingrained that there is no social memory of its origin. The common law *cannot remember* its origins. Custom transforms into law organically, naturally, and imperceptibly whenever there has never been a frustration of that habituated expectation framework. Each *judicial* repetition of some such element of the common law becomes, thereby, a repetition of other repetitions, with the (if it can be so called) *primal* repetition being constitutively inaccessible to the common law's consciousness.

Even key historical moments in the development of the common law can ultimately only be considered as, at most, *prior repetitions*. As such, the common law generally shuns even the thought of *creativity:* difference (creation) is continually subordinated to repetition (non-creation). For example, William Blackstone, discussing the origins of the common law or *Lex non Scripta*, references Alfred of Wessex's law-code or *domboc* from the 9th century (before time of memory) as a key blueprint for subsequent legal developments. Taking this for illustrative purposes: while the *domboc* is not what we would recognise as a comprehensive articulation of the common law, it was 'an attempt to impose uniformity in some limited fields' (Baker, 2019: 5) and had important historical influence (see Hudson, 2017). The *domboc* itself seeks to connect the law code to the deep past, though as a law *code* experimenting with the practice of authoritatively marking law with the sign of sovereignty, it does so through constructing a historical account which explains legal authority through a chronology of religious and political lineages. As Anya Adair notes (2021: 24), Alfred's temporal manoeuvre seeks to establish legal authority such that Alfred's authority is temporally coincident with local *and* biblical history: the 'preface to the *domboc* settles its negotiation of time and authority via its positioning of Alfred as lawmaker and its calculated disavowal that Alfredian lawmaking is an *ex nihilo* act of royal authority'. Its narration of an interconnected English legal history alongside a biblical one is one where the Mosaic laws of Exodus are brought into historical connection to the present, such that 'God speaks from ancient Egypt directly to the audience of the present moment: originary past and legal present are brought into close communion' (Adair, 2021: 16). But even this grounding of legal authority does not reach as far as the common law: Blackstone notes (2016: 51) that the *actual* foundation or ground of the customs and maxims expressed in the *domboc* are of 'higher antiquity than memory or history can reach', describing the "goodness" of a custom as being directly related to the extent to which it has been in operation time out of mind, 'or, in the solemnity of our legal phrase, time whereof the memory of man runneth not to the contrary'. CLT will locate the *source* or *origin* of the common law beyond the reach of recorded history, such that this origin is constitutively outside the common law's consciousness.

To be more schematic from what we have said thus far: a rhythmanalysis of common law, focusing on its role in the establishment of juridico-political continuity, is concerned with how the common law functions to bind a milieu to particular histories, situating the milieu in a particular temporal present, as the ground from which the milieu can develop or transform. The relationship the common law establishes to the past and the future is one which, by tendency, slows the pace of transformation such that juridico-political continuity to the purported deep past is respected and maintained. The temporal texture of common law as it pertains to the *retentional* element of the establishment of juridico-political continuity has two axes: it is both a system of *memory* in the sense that it acts as a repository of those previously mentioned ingrained customs, practices, and expectations, as well as a system of *forgetting* which only remembers what it selects and which grounds the authoritative status of custom in its very lack of a discrete historical (spatio-temporal) location.

The common law as a system of forgetting pertains to the common law move to situate the source or origin of law outside of recorded history. This (non-)origin of the common law is precisely that which the common law *cannot* experience ("time out of mind"). As such, in practice, the only models for the common law to imitate are prior repetitions. This can be termed the common law's *default of origin*, origin in default, or aporetic origin, a term and approach we are developing from Stiegler's discussion concerning the origins of the human in relation to the technical (Stiegler, 1998: 134–172; Crogan, 2009; Turner, 2019). The invocation of custom or time immemorial anchors itself in that which, of necessity, cannot be discretely remembered, transforming the descriptive fact of prior repetitions (as custom, habit) into self-grounding normatively salient reasons for yet more repetitions. The common law's operation has this essentially self-referential character: legal authority pertains to repetitions and repetitions of repetitions, of which we have no access to the primal repetition; the purposive movement of the common law, and in every daily iteration, must in practice constitutively forget its default of origin to ensure its quotidian continuation. To the extent that the common law engages in the sort of "blind imitation" James Kent accused it of, it nonetheless constitutes a system of forgetting *in the service of* establishing juridico-political continuity. If the non-origin or contingency of the law were *not* forgotten in everyday life, this would dissolve the very expectation frameworks legal institutions and practice serve to produce. In other words, the common law's default of origin and operation as a system of forgetting its non-origins has a practical function in the establishment of juridico-political continuity in the present through binding the milieu to the purported deep past of the milieu.

It would not be fair, however, to reduce the common law's operation to this element of blindness or as a system of forgetting. The second element of the common law's retentional character in the establishment of juridico-political continuity pertains to the ways in which it *also* establishes a system of memory of that which is within its field of visibility. The primary mechanism through which the common law adapts (or not) to changing circumstances is, of course, through the *case*, and the common law is in significant respects a history of cases and precedents, which are its own internal system of memory. The case, in practice, is always particular, different, and singular, contingent (McNeilly and Stapleton, 2017), and the judicial role in CLT will involve the process through which the *singular* case can be integrated into the *generality* of some legal rule or principle, and through this ultimately into the generality of the legal system itself. This integration with the legal system "itself" on a case-by-case basis *is* the central method through which the common law facilitates the contraction of juridico-political continuity. To establish juridico-political continuity, the common law must manage the discontinuity that the singularity of the case threatens to pose by enlisting the case within its system of past, present, and future. When confronting the contingency of the present case in all its particularity, judges must consider the past such that their judgment will be consonant with this past, but also so this judgment produces protentional force such that any future repetition of potential similar particularities can be more quickly subsumed into the legal system.

Precedent is the definitive, although not only, common law method for dealing with the vast majority of case particularities such that they become integrated into the narrative of juridico-political continuity. Precedent in the common law can be treated in narrow and broad senses (Bankowski et al., 2016: 323). The narrow sense pertains to that part of the case which is legally binding, and judicial reasoning will become concerned in such instances with determining what, in a previous case, counts as precedent and what does not. In the broader sense, a precedent is a prior court decision which has some 'legally significant analogy to the case now before a court' (loc. cit.). The common law is conservative to the extent that it leans towards *repetition* prejudicially via *stare decisis*, but *what* is repeated and *how* it is repeated must remain, within bounds, open to the future (towards, that is, *difference*) such that new *expressions* of the law can be given in relation to the contingency of new cases presenting new problems and changing technosocial conditions which can transform how these problems are understood. The history of the common law thus in this sense both constrains (limits) and enables (produces interpretive opportunities) its protentionality. The case is both a vector of continuity and variation. The case's singularity is that which enables its potential operation as a vector of variation, where the contingent event can be met with experimental and creative forms of jurisprudence, where even Deleuze, for example, suggested with some enthusiasm that a jurisprudence proceeded by singularities offered the promise of a truly inventive jurisprudence (Deleuze, 1990: 209–210; Saunders, 2012). Nonetheless, in the majority of cases, even that which is seemingly "new" in the common law (such as some new formulation of legal content) is produced with reference to the past, whether this be in case law, with reference to historical principles, or through the very legal form of the case itself, such that even when there is variation, it is a constrained and managed form of variation *within* juridico-political continuity. In other words, while Deleuze appears attracted to the inventive possibilities of a jurisprudence which creatively confronted the singularity of the case, such openness to the future is not generally a temporal posture common law courts are likely to adopt, due to the fact such an inventive jurisprudence would foreseeably disturb expectation frameworks in the milieu. The common law's attachment and adherence to expectation frameworks have varied. In a rigid form of *stare decisis*, the courts have considered it better to repeat errors in judgment for the purpose of preserving such expectation frameworks and juridico-political continuity, as with *London Street Tramways v London City Council*, where the House of Lords affirmed that their own legal determinations bind even themselves in the future such that only an act of Parliament could set aside precedent (Pugsley, 1996). In contrast, looser interpretations of *stare decisis* do not so rigidly bind the courts to repetition and allow for the potential (although limited) for a precedent to be overruled in certain conditions (see *Practice Statement (Judicial Precedent)*).

Previously, we noted that the common law generally shuns creativity, such that difference (creation) must continually be subordinated to repetition (non-creation). But this does not mean the common law does not have its own *modality* of creativity proper to its internal system of memory. For example, *if* the application of precedent would lead to some putatively unreasonable outcome, the common law technique will lean towards *distinguishing* a case such that the legally significant analogy will not obtain, and an alternative mode of reasoning will be evinced such that the expectation framework of that precedent is maintained without producing what the court considers to be the unreasonable outcome that the precedent would have had. *Distinguishing* is a modality of judicial creativity which reproduces juridico-political continuity and ostensibly respects the expectation frameworks set by precedent. A second common mode of judicial creativity is that of *analogy* or analogical reasoning. Analogy will prolong or extend some precedent to the particularities of a present case. In general terms, precedents can bind when there is sufficient overlap between some case in the past and the case before the courts in the present such that the *ratio decidendi* for the former is taken as applying, or that it ought to apply, to the latter. Analogy is not the simple application of precedent, and it pertains to the often slow and piecemeal evolution of the common law, putting old precedents to the "test" of the new and the particular through consideration of the concrete case. Relevant here is Hale's (1971: 40) famous comparison of the development of the common law to the ship of the Argonauts. He argued that, even after a long voyage which required adjustments, modifications, and fixes to the ship, we would still say it is the *same* ship, and so we must in just the same way say that the common law is the *same* despite its own adjustments, modifications, and fixes.

From a rhythmanalytical perspective, the "sameness" or "identity" of objects are considered as aspects of a dramatic and unfolding becoming made up of repetitions, contractions, and deviations the common law is not one thing, but rather a set of loops, patterns, undulations, and processes which in practice are produced and reproduced as having stability over time. The maintenance of apparent continuity is, this is to say, a result of continual judicial creativity. Maintenance *must* include transformation from a processual perspective, but the work of the common law is to efface transformation to maintain the semblance of sameness and stability of juridico-political continuity. The technique of analogy is a creative process through which the common law maintains juridico-political continuity despite its piecemeal and context-driven developments and changes, effacing its creativity only by officially recognising what is already part of the system of memory. Through analogy, difference is transformed into sameness such that the particularities of new cases become, through the process of legal reasoning and judgment, transformed into new iterations of what the common law *already knows* through its system of memory. In the practices of distinguishing and of analogy, the articulation of legal argument and the making of legal judgment are effectuated in terms of and in constitutive relation to already-existing precedent, enabling the common law to incorporate difference and contingency through its already-constituted system of memory. The common law's creativity, this is to say, is to efface its own creativity in judgments which are produced such that they are integrated into the narrative of juridico-political continuity.

While we may be able to pick out snapshots at different chronological moments and be able to identify differences in legal doctrine, to focus on these snapshots as evidence of difference underplays the "insensible" nature of these changes as they occur. As Parker notes (2011b: 601), such a partial approach to change is the common law method of collapsing identity and difference, that is, through which legal judgment (and its techniques) functions to mediate the threat of discontinuity posed by the case in order to assimilate difference into sameness and maintain juridico-political continuity. This concrete flexibility of the common law enables it to integrate the potentially singular and disruptive case into the generality of the legal system, and this bottom-up case-by-case method of producing and reproducing the legal system over time is a key feature of its power in channelling disruptions in the milieu into the very motor of legal continuity (Shapiro, 2011: 198–199; Strauss, 1996).

Lex Scripta, as we discussed previously, has authoritative force automatically and is a form of rapid social normativity unmoored to the past. *Lex non Scripta* is slower, moored to a past that, by definition, it cannot sense. While it is often the case that the two are considered as operating in some form of tension, as if positive law and the common law operated at odds, it is rather that they constitute two distinct *speeds* of juridico-political normativity which dynamically operate in the service of juridico-political continuity and its reproduction. Statute law has an openness to the future which enables it to respond to transforming conditions rapidly, but the common law's orientation is primarily in the service of the continual stabilisation of expectation frameworks, and therefore to the past, often slowing down the rapidity of statute by filtering it through common law reasoning. Rather than operating in opposition, it is rather that they interact to maintain the fragile continuation of social reproduction in everyday life.

§15.3 Repetition and Difference

We noted at the top of this chapter that the central purpose of this section is to begin to outline why law ought to be taken more seriously by the rhythmanalyst. As far as we are aware, while much rhythmanalysis has engaged in important work on, say, how power relations are instituted, reproduced, habituated to, and performed at the level of the everyday, limited work has been done in relation to the *legal everyday*: those everyday legal obligations and expectation frameworks which structure and constrain, but also enable and produce, certain types of social relations. The legal everyday, however, cannot be approached without an analysis of the processes through which these expectation frameworks and obligations, as well as legal order, are produced and enforced. Legal order, expectation frameworks, and quotidian legal obligations are elements of what we have been here calling *juridico-political continuity*. The question of *lawmaking* and the distinct but interrelated temporalities of statute and common law are key vehicles through which such juridico-political continuity is continually produced and reproduced (in addition to the work of, e.g., administrative agencies, police, prisons, and alternative forms of dispute resolution). Such a focus allows us to pursue rhythmanalytical attention to the everyday in such a way that connects the everyday to larger scale dynamics. This, as we have discussed on a number of occasions, is vital for the rhythmanalyst: not just the everyday at the level of this or that individual's experience, but how *this* or *that* everyday is constituted in relation to other processes, whether they be cosmological, ecological, biological, technosocial, or specifically *juridical*.

Stabilised expectation frameworks in everyday life enable planning and new protentional trajectories. *Lex Scripta* and *Lex non Scripta* work together in the creation of an entire framework of expectations: rooting the milieu in some putative deep origin as with the common law, but at one and the same time providing an ordered sequence of movements or ritual through which the milieu can create its own future in response to contingency, as with statute law. While their rhythms are distinct, their dynamic interactions are the stuff of juridico-political continuity, stability, and indeed *legitimacy* in the milieu, such that both can stake a claim to their processes and practices as having some special significant relationship to the *ground* or *source* of justified authority (common law in the deep past or in custom of a "people" or "territory", statute law in how agreement was achieved among those recently democratically approved by citizens in the most recent election cycle). Our contention here is that this perspective – focusing on the question of how juridico-political continuity is established and continually re-established – is an innovative one offered by rhythmanalysis. When living everyday life within more or less stable political and legal contexts, we subsist in a form of juridico-political continuity, the constitution of which the rhythmanalyst must take seriously, given the formative character it has on the shaping of everyday life. Juridico-political continuity must therefore become an object of more detailed concern for rhythmanalysts in their analysis of everyday life.

There is much detail we could not explore here, and it is hoped that this investigation has helped raise further exploratory questions. But it is important to note two final points before concluding this chapter. First, it is important to note that our focus on *continuity* is not at all meant to undermine the notion of *discontinuity*. Legal institutions and practices, we have suggested, are in the business of producing at least the sense of continuity in everyday life. However, an entire rhythmanalysis of juridico-political *discontinuity* remains to be done, exploring the rhythms of, for example, resistance, revolutions, riots, and so forth. Long-term studies on the ebbing and flowing of juridico-political continuities and discontinuities in different milieus is one potential avenue of further research to explore on this point. Secondly, and relatedly, given our analysis concerning how both common law and statute law operate to consolidate and reproduce juridico-political continuity over the long-term (beyond this or that election cycle), it is posited that it is through these longer timescales that the rhythmanalyst can think in more detail about not just the consolidation and sedimentation of habits and practices in everyday life, but also their transformation. Rhythmanalysis has its focus on the everyday, but it remains to be seen whether it can offer a new way of approaching the creation of *new* forms of juridico-political continuity in our future milieus. Although vital, rhythmanalysis cannot consign itself to the critique of existing milieus and their operation, but ought to open itself up to experimenting with inventing new milieus and new ways of life in relationship to our biorhythmic, cosmorhythmic, and technosocial-rhythmic worlds.

References

Adair, A. 2021. Narratives of Authority: The Earliest Old English Law-code Prefaces. *Law and Humanities*, 15(1): 4–24.

Ağca-Varoğlu, F. G. 2021. "Staying at Home": A Rhythmanalysis of Self-Quarantine. In *The Societal Impacts of COVID-19: A Transnational Perspective*. Eds. V. Bozkurt, G. Dawes, H. Gulerce and P. Westenbroek. Istanbul: Istanbul University Press, pp. 45–62.

Baker, J. 2019. *An Introduction to English Legal History*. Oxford: Oxford University Press.

Bankowski, Z., MacCormick, D. N. and Marshall, G. 2016. Precedent in the United Kingdom. In *Interpreting Precedents: A Comparative Study*. Eds. D. N. MacCormick and R. S. Summers. London: Routledge, pp. 315–354.

Benyon-Jones, S. M. and Grabham, E. (Eds.). 2019. *Law and Time*. Oxon: Routledge.

Bingham, T. 2011. *The Rule of Law*. London: Penguin Books.

BIPM. 2019. Mise en pratique for the definition of the second in the SI. www.bipm. org/documents/20126/41489667/SI-App2-second.pdf/3c76fec8-04d9-f484-5c3c-a2e280a0f248?version=1.12&t=1643724477633 [accessed 20 April 2022].

Birth, K. 2019. Standards in the Shadows for Everyone to See: The Supranational Regulation of Time and the Concern over Temporal Pluralism. In *Law and Time*. Eds. S. M. Benyon-Jones and E. Grabham. Oxon: Routledge, pp. 196–211.

Blackstone, W. 2016. *Commentaries on the Laws of England: Book I: Of the Rights of Persons*. Oxford: Oxford University Press.

Blair, A., Karsten, L. and Leopold, J. 2001. Britain and the Working Time Regulations. *Politics*, 21(1): 40–46.

Case C-344/19 *DJ v Radiotelevizija Slovenija* ECLI:EU:C:2021:182.

Case C-580/19 *RJ v Stadt Offenbach am Main* ECLI:EU:C:2021:183.

Chester, G. 2015. Wait a Second . . . 2015 Will Be a Little Longer. *CHIPS: The Department of the Navy's Information Technology Magazine*. https://www.doncio. navy.mil/(iok2uj55403hahactawnmbiw)/CHIPS/ArticleDetails.aspx?ID=6471 [accessed 08/09/22]

Chowdhury, T. 2020. *Time, Temporality and Legal Judgment*. Oxon: Routledge.

Coaffee, J. 2021. *The War on Terror and the Normalisation of Urban Security*. London: Routledge.

Coole, D. 2007. Experiencing Discourse: Corporeal Communicators and the Embodiment of Power. *British Journal of Politics and International Relations*, 9: 413–433.

Crogan, P. 2009. The Duck and the Philosopher: Rhythms of Editing and Thinking between Bernard Stiegler and *The Ister. Transformation: Journal of Media, Culture & Technology*, 17.

Curtis v March. 157 E.R. 719 (1858).

Dakka, F. and Davitti, D. 2022. International Human Rights Law and Time-Space at Sea: A Rhythmanalysis of Prosecuting Search and Rescue. In *The Times and Temporalities of International Human Rights Law*. Eds. K. McNeilly and B. Warwick. Oxford: Hart, pp. 121–139.

Davies, M. 2017. *Asking the Law Question*. Sydney: Law Book Company.

Deleuze, G. 1990. *Pourparlers, 1972–1990*. Paris: Minuit.

De Wandeler, K., Mendis, R. M., Nanayakkara, S. M. and Vasudevan, M. 2020. Rhythmanalysis of Life During Physical Distancing for Covid-19: Sri Lankans in Brussels, Belgium. *Cities People Places: An International Journal on Urban Environments*, 4(2): 1–24.

De Wilde, M. 2015. Just Trust Us: A Short History of Emergency Powers and Constitutional Change. *Comparative Legal History*, 3(1): 110–130.

Dworkin, R. 2002. *Sovereign Virtue: The Theory and Practice of Equality*. Cambridge, MA: Harvard University Press.

Dyson, F. W. 1916. Standard Time in Ireland. *The Observatory*, 39: 467–468.

Ellen Street Estates Ltd v Minister of Health [1934] 1 KB 590.

Foran, M. 2021. The Emergency Paradox: Constitutional Interpretation in Times of Crisis. *Edinburgh Law Review*, 25(1): 118–124.

Genosko, G. and Hegarty, P. 2020. Smearing Time: Critical Temporality and Corporate Ontology. *Time & Society*, 29(4): 1009–1023.

Goodrich, P. 2016. Melancholegalism: Black Letter Theory and the Temporality of Law. *Crisis & Critique*, 3(2): 184–203.

Gordon, G. 2018. Railway Clocks. In *International Law's Objects*. Eds. J. Hohmann and D. Joyce. Oxford: Oxford University Press, pp. 387–398.

Gray, K. J. and Gray, S. F. 2009. *Elements of Land Law*. Oxford: Oxford University Press.

Hale, M. 1971. *A History of the Common Law of England*. Ed. C. M. Gray. Chicago, IL: University of Chicago Press.

Heaney, C. 2022. Changing Time/Timing Changes: Daylight Saving and the Politics of Time. *Strathclyde Law Blog*. www.strath.ac.uk/humanities/lawschool/blog/changingtimetimingchangesdaylightsavingthepoliticsoftime/ [accessed 10 September 2022].

Henderson v Reynolds, 10 SE 734 (Ga 1889).

Hertz, R. and Leuffen, D. 2011. Too Big to Run? Analysing the Impact of Enlargement on the Speed of EU Decision-making. *European Union Politics*, 12(2): 193–215.

Hobbes, T. 1996. *Leviathan*. Cambridge: Cambridge University Press.

Hobbes, T. 2008. *Writings on Common Law and Hereditary Right*. Eds. A. Cromartie and Q. Skinner. Oxford: Clarendon Press.

Holmes, O. W. 1995. The Path of the Law. In *Vol. 3, The Collected Works of Justice Holmes: Complete Public Writings and Selected Judicial Opinions of Oliver Wendell Holmes*. Ed. S. M. Novick. Chicago, IL: University of Chicago Press.

Hudson, J. 2017. *The Formation of the Common Law: Law and Society in England from King Alfred to Magna Carta*. London: Routledge.

Keenan, S. 2019. Making Land Liquid: On Time and Title Registration. In *Law and Time*. Eds. S. M. Benyon-Jones and E. Grabham. Oxon: Routledge, pp. 145–161.

Kent, J. 1840. *Commentaries on American Law*. New York: E. B. Clayton.

Kwapińska, K. 2022. Technological Evolution and the Political Agency of Artificial Intelligence from the Perspective of General Organology and Universal Organicism. *Információs Társadalom*, XXII(2): 57–71.

Lefebvre, H. 1988. Toward a Leftist Cultural Politics: Remarks Occasioned by the Centenary of Marx's Death. Trans. D. Reifman. In *Marxism and the Interpretation of Culture*. Ed. C. Nelson. Urbana, IL: University of Illinois Press, pp. 75–88.

Lefebvre, H. 2013. *Rhythmanalysis: Space, Time and Everyday Life*. Trans. S. Elden and G. Moore. London: Bloomsbury Academic.

Lefebvre, H. 2014. Critique of Everyday Life, Volume III: From Modernity to Modernism (Towards a Metaphilosophy of Daily Life). Trans. G. Elliot. In *Critique of Everyday Life: The One Volume Edition*. London: Verso, pp. 653–842.

Lightbown, S. and Smith, B. 2009. Parliamentary Tends: Statistics about Parliament. Research Paper 09/69, House of Commons Library.

London Street Tramways Co v London City Council [1898] AC 375.

Mawani, R. 2015. The Times of Law. *Law & Social Inquiry*, 40(1): 253–263.

McNeilly, K. and Stapleton, P. 2017. Judging the Singular: Towards a Contingent Practice of Improvisation in Law. *Critical Studies in Improvisation*, 12(1).

McNeilly, K. and Warwick, B. (Eds.). 2022. *The Times and Temporalities of International Human Rights Law*. Oxford: Hart.

Neocleous, M. 2006. The Problem with Normality: Taking Exception to "Permanent Emergency". *Alternatives*, 31: 191–213.

Novak, P. 2017. Border Rhythms. In *Timespace and International Migration*. Eds. E. Mavroudi, B. Page and A. Christou. Cheltenham: Edward Elgar, pp. 61–76.

Nowak, T. 2018. The Turbulent Life of the Working Time Directive. *Maastricht Journal of European and Comparative Law*, 25(1): 118–129.

O'Connell, R. 2012. The Right to Work in the ECHR. *European Human Rights Law Review*, 2: 176–190.

Parker, K. M. 2011a. *Common Law, History, and Democracy in America, 1790–1900: Legal Thought Before Modernism*. Cambridge: Cambridge University Press.

Parker, K. M. 2011b. Law "In" and "As" History: The Common Law in the American Polity, 1790–1900. *U.C. Irvine Law Review*, 1(3): 587–609.

Parrish, J. 2002. Litigating Time in America at the Turn of the Twentieth Century. *Akron Law Review*, 36(1): 1–47.

Paterson, J. 1894. *The Intoxicating Liquor Licensing Acts, 1872, 1874*. London: Shaw & Sons.

Philippopoulos-Mihalopoulos, A. 2015. *Spatial Justice: Body, Lawscape, Atmosphere*. London: Routledge.

Pocock, J. G. A. 1987. *The Ancient Constitution and the Feudal Law: A Study of English Historical Thought in the Seventeenth Century*. Cambridge: Cambridge University Press.

Postema, G. J. 1986. *Bentham and the Common Law Tradition*. Oxford: Clarendon Press.

Postema, G. J. 2015. Jurisprudence, the Sociable Science. *Virginia Law Review*, 101(4): 903–917.

Practice Statement (Judicial Precedent) [1996] 1 WLR 1234.

Pugsley, D. 1996. London Tramways (1898). *The Journal of Legal History*, 17(2): 172–184.

Rai, S. M. 2010. Analysing Ceremony and Ritual in Parliament. *The Journal of Legislative Studies*, 16(3): 284–297.

Rawls, J. 1993. *Political Liberalism*. New York: Columbia University Press.

Roberts, S. 2013. *Order and Dispute: An Introduction to Legal Anthropology*. New Orleans, LA: Quid Pro Books.

Rooney, D. 2021. *About Time: A History of Civilization in Twelve Clocks*. New York: W. W. Norton & Company.

Rooney, D. and Nye, J. 2009. "Greenwich Observatory Time for the Public Benefit": Standard Time and Victorian Networks of Regulation. *The British Journal for the History of Science*, 42(1): 5–30.

Rose, E. 2018. The New Politics of Time. *International Journal of Comparative Labour Law and Industrial Relations*, 34(4): 373–394.

Rose, J. L. 2016. *Free Time*. Princeton, NJ: Princeton University Press.

Saunders, D. 2012. Cases against Transcendence: Gilles Deleuze and Bruno Latour in Defence of Law. In *Deleuze and Law*. Eds. L. de Sutter and K. McGee. Edinburgh: Edinburgh University Press, pp. 185–203.

Shapiro, S. 2011. *Legality*. Cambridge: The Belknap Press.

Sobel, D. 2011. *Longitude*. London: Harper Perennial.

Stiegler, B. 1998. *Technics and Time 1: The Fault of Epimetheus*. Trans. R. Beardsworth and G. Collins. Stanford, CA: Stanford University Press.

Strauss, D. 1996. Common Law Constitutionalism. *University of Chicago Law Review*, 63(3): 877–935.

Thomas, M. W. 1948. *The Early Factory Legislation*. Leigh-on-Sea: The Thames Bank Publishing Company.

Toshkov, D. D. 2017. The Impact of the Eastern Enlargement on the Decision-making Capacity of the European Union. *Journal of European Public Policy*, 24(2): 177–196.

Turner, B. 2019. From Resistance to Invention in the Politics of the Impossible: Bernard Stiegler's Political Reading of Maurice Blanchot. *Contemporary Political Theory*, 18(1): 43–64.

Wallace, S. 2020. Derogations from the European Convention on Human Rights: The Case for Reform. *Human Rights Law Review*, 20(4): 769–796.

Working Time Directive 2003/88/EC.

Zahn, R. 2021. Does Stand-by Time Count as Working Time? The Court of Justice Gives Guidance in *DJ v Radiotelevizija Slovenija* and *RJ v Stadt Offenbach am Main*. *European Papers*, 6(1): 121–124.

Zayani, M. 1999. Introduction to Rhythmanalysis. *Rethinking Marxism*, 11(1): 1–4.

Conclusion
Repeat to Fade

§16 Recursion

This book has been an *experimental* rhythmanalysis that can, we hope, be approached primarily as an *invitation* to explore the creative and critical potentials of this diverse and plural methodological field. In addition to the work of *criticism*, rhythmanalysis can be deployed as a method of *critique*. As Iain MacKenzie (2004: 40–41) discusses, whereas the work of *criticism* is situated within a particular house of concepts (concerned with internal 'lacunae or inconsistencies' as well as philosophical 'fine-tuning' therein), the work of *critique* is concerned with concept-creation and of building new houses of concepts or new conceptual milieus. *While criticism is an invitation to criticise, critique is an invitation to create.* MacKenzie here highlights what Deleuze and Guattari note on this point, in which the latter criticises the static or "petrified" use of concepts treated as if they were rigid frameworks:

> Nothing positive is done, nothing at all, in the domains of either criticism or history, when we are content to brandish ready-made old concepts like skeletons intended to intimidate any creation, without seeing that the ancient philosophers from whom we borrow them were already doing what we would like to prevent modern philosophers from doing: they were creating their concepts, and they were not happy just to clean and scrape bones like the critic and historian of our time. Even the history of philosophy is completely without interest if it does not undertake to awaken a dormant concept and to play it again on a new stage, even if this comes at the price of turning it against itself.
>
> (1994: 83)

DOI: 10.4324/9781003350231-5

Rhythmanalysis, if it is to be engaged in *critique*, must experiment and create. For Miller (2004: 20), 'Rhythm science uses an endless recontextualizing as a core compositional strategy', but what further strategies can be invented remains an open question. The domain of law has been focused on here as one such avenue of such experimentation and creation, to which we have sketched out an initial pattern.

By orienting our experiment through the rhythm-law nexus, each chapter in the book explored this to attempt to gather the materials for conceptual creation. In the Introduction, the temporal ordering of everyday life passed through the Benedictine monks, the imagined prison timetable, as well as Crowley's factory workers. The production and ordering of social time and everyday life were the objects of concern. Critically, law and its relationship to the milieu require(d) conceptualisation. We offered elements of such an account, which drew us, in Chapter 1, to investigate in more detail some of the multiple directions rhythmanalysis can take us (biorhythms, cosmorhythms, technosocial rhythms), as well as some of the recent work in this area. In Chapter 2, we tried to survey some of the rich etymological history of the notion of rhythm as from Ancient Greece, where rhythm becomes associated closely in Plato as an ordered sequence of movement, bound and regulated by number. The reading we offered was composed to highlight the significance of rhythm in grasping the *cosmos* and in crafting the *nomos*. Chapter 3 approached the rhythm-law nexus in conversations concerned with the ordering of social time, whether in the everyday life of standardised and working time or at the more diffuse and spread-out temporal level of juridico-political continuity through which the durative bonds of social practices are tied together.

Lefebvre's ambitions with his own *Rhythmanalysis*, as mentioned at the opening of that text, were to 'found a science, a new field of knowledge [*savoir*]: the analysis of rhythms, with practical consequences' (2013: 3), building on the work of Lúcio Alberto Pinheiro dos Santos (1931), but also Nietzsche and Bachelard. It remains to be seen whether such ambitions can be fulfilled. In an alternative formulation much closer to our own, Lefebvre and Régulier elsewhere frame their rhythmanalytical contribution in a two-fold manner. First, they propose what we would term *concept creation*, constructing rhythmanalysis from its diverse instruments ('the theory of measurement, the history of music, chronobiology and even cosmological theories' (Lefebvre and Régulier, 2013: 106). Second, through this construction and related analyses, they describe the articulation of *materials to sample*, to be 'taken up and carried further than before by others' (loc. cit.). In such sampling and endless recontextualisation, rhythmanalysis offers not simply new *critical* possibilities, but the invention of new conceptual milieus and new modalities of *critique*.

References

Deleuze, G. and Guattari, F. 1994. *What Is Philosophy?* Trans. G. Burchill and H. Tomlinson. London: Verso.

dos Santos, L. P. 1931. *Ritmanálise*. Rio de Janeiro: Société de Psychologie et de Philosophie.

Lefebvre, H. 2013. *Rhythmanalysis: Space, Time and Everyday Life*. Trans. S. Elden and G. Moore. London: Bloomsbury Academic.

Lefebvre, H., and Régulier, C., 'Attempt at the Rhythmanalysis of Mediterranean Cities', in Lefebvre, H. 2013. *Rhythmanalysis: Space, Time and Everyday Life*. Trans. S. Elden and G. Moore. London: Bloomsbury Academic, pp. 93–106.

MacKenzie, I. 2004. *The Idea of Pure Critique*. London: Continuum.

Miller, P. D. 2004. *Rhythm Science*. Cambridge, MA: MIT Press.

Index

For Product Safety Concerns and Information please contact our EU
representative GPSR@taylorandfrancis.com
Taylor & Francis Verlag GmbH, Kaufingerstraße 24, 80331 München, Germany

www.ingramcontent.com/pod-product-compliance
Lightning Source LLC
Chambersburg PA
CBHW061336220326
41599CB00026B/5214